DRIVING STANDARDS AGENCY
SAFE DRIVING FOR LIFE™

THEORY TEST
EXTRA
the OFFICIAL DSA GUIDE

London: TSO

Prepared by the Learning Materials Section of the Driving Standards Agency

© Crown Copyright 2008

Previously known as *Theory Test Companion*
First published 2001
Second edition 2003

New title *Theory Test Extra*
Fourth edition 2008
Second impression 2008

ISBN 9780115529351

A CIP catalogue record for this book is available from the British Library.

Other titles in the Driving Skills series

The Official DSA Guide to Driving - the essential skills
The Official DSA Theory Test for Car Drivers
The Official DSA Theory Test for Car Drivers (CD-Rom)
Helping Learners to Practise - the official DSA guide
The Official DSA Guide to Learning to Drive
Prepare for your Practical Driving Test DVD
DSA Driving Theory DVD Quiz

The Official DSA Guide to Riding - the essential skills
The Official DSA Theory Test for Motorcyclists
The Official DSA Theory Test for Motorcyclists (CD-Rom)
The Official DSA Guide to Learning to Ride
Better Biking - the Official DSA Training Aid (DVD)

The Official DSA Guide to Driving Buses and Coaches
The Official DSA Guide to Driving Goods Vehicles
The Official DSA Theory Test for Drivers of Large Vehicles
The Official DSA Theory Test for Drivers of Large Vehicles (CD-Rom)
Driver CPC - the Official DSA Guide for Professional Bus and Coach Drivers

The Official DSA Guide to Tractor and Specialist Vehicle Driving Tests

The Official DSA Guide to Hazard Perception (DVD)

75% recycled
This book is printed
on 75% recycled paper

CONTENTS

Introduction

Do I take my theory test before I sign up for driving lessons?

No, not at all, in fact you should be having driving lessons as you're studying for the theory test. This will allow you to put what you're learning into practice on the road. It's important that you know about safety and regulations whilst you're learning to drive.

Your test certificate only lasts for two years. If you don't pass your practical test within this time you'll have to start again.

How do I find an instructor?

Choose an Approved Driving Instructor (ADI), as they will have reached a standard set by the Driving Standards Agency (DSA). They're graded 1-6, 4 being the standard, 5 and 6 reaching a higher standard of instruction. Make enquiries about this before you make a decision. Ask your friends about their instructor, but choose someone you're comfortable with. You can always change your instructor if this isn't the case.

"YOU CAN ALWAYS CHANGE YOUR INSTRUCTOR"

What is the theory test like?

The theory test is a computer-based test and consists of two parts: multiple choice questions and a hazard perception part. The questions test your knowledge of driving theory: you touch the screen to select the correct answer or answers. The hazard perception part uses film clips to test your hazard awareness. You click on a mouse button when you see a developing hazard to which you, as a driver, need to respond. You must pass both parts of the test in order to pass the theory test.

Why do I need this book?

You'll be asked 50 questions during the multiple choice part of your test. You'll have to get at least 43 correct to pass this part of the theory test. It's important you're well prepared or else you could be wasting money by having to take the test more than once. Anyway, being well prepared should make you safer on the road which could mean that you'll pass your driving test sooner.

How to use this book

The test covers various subjects and all of them are covered in this book. You'll notice that they're colour coded for easy reference. The questions you'll be asked are based on these, so if you study this book you won't find the multiple choice part of the test difficult at all.

Questions in the test are based on information taken from the three books listed below.

Icon references in the margin let you refer to the original text. This gives you information in more detail.

HC
80, p64 ▶ rule/page number in *The Official Highway Code*

D
7 ▶ part in *Driving - the essential skills*

KYTS
80 ▶ page number in *Know Your Traffic Signs*

We have provided you with two revision tests on pages 90 and 100 so that you can practice. You can also study the *Official Theory Test for Car Drivers* which shows you all the questions, together with the answers and a brief explanation.

1 Alertness

"DRIVING SAFELY TAKES A LOT OF CONCENTRATION. LOOK AROUND CONSTANTLY AND BE ALERT"

Observation

Driving safely takes a lot of concentration. Look around constantly and assess the changing situations as you drive.

Be aware of traffic all around you. Before you carry out any manoeuvre you should

HC
159-161 ▶

D
4 ▶

- use your mirrors to assess how your actions will affect traffic behind you
- look around for a final check
- signal if necessary.

If you can't see behind when reversing, ask a reliable person to guide you.

If you can't see when emerging from a junction because your view is obstructed by parked cars, move forward slowly and carefully until you can get a proper view.

HC
163 ▶

D
7 ▶

Be particularly careful before you overtake. Ensure that

- you have a clear view of the road ahead – there shouldn't be any bends or dips
- you have enough time to complete the manoeuvre safely.

It's also important for other road users to know you're there.

HC
113-115 ▶

- When it starts to get dark, switch on your lights, even if the street lights aren't on.
- Where you can't be seen, such as at a hump-back bridge, consider using your horn.

Anticipation and awareness

Look at the road signs and markings; these give you information about any hazards. You should

- follow their advice
- slow down if necessary.

Watch other road users. Try to anticipate their actions so you're ready if you need to slow down or change direction.

When turning right onto a dual carriageway, first check that the central reservation is wide enough for your vehicle.

Be aware of other, more vulnerable road users. Watch out for

- pedestrians, especially where they may be hidden or approaching a crossing
- cyclists, always pass slowly and leave plenty of room
- motorcyclists, who may be obscured by your windscreen pillar.

If you're approaching traffic lights that have been green for some time, be prepared to stop because they may change.

However well prepared you are, you may still have to stop quickly in an emergency. Keep both hands on the wheel as you brake to keep control of your vehicle.

Concentration

Always plan your journey so you

- know what route you need to take
- have regular rest stops.

You'll not be able to concentrate properly if you're tired. It's particularly easy to feel sleepy on a motorway, so

- don't drive continuously for more than two hours
- ensure you've a supply of fresh air
- if you feel tired, leave at the next exit. Find a safe place to stop and have a short nap.

◄ **D** 6

◄ **KYTS** 10, 62

◄ **HC** 204-218

◄ **D** 10

◄ **D** 6

◄ **D** 5

◄ **HC** 91, 262

◄ **D** 1

Distraction

D 1

HC 149-150

Don't let passengers distract you. If you argue with them it will take your mind off driving. Loud music and high spirits may mean you're having fun, but it can be distracting for the driver, and could end in disaster.

You can also be distracted by

- objects hanging in the car
- tuning your radio or inserting a cassette or CD
- looking at a map
- talking into a microphone.

Just taking your eyes off the road for a second could be disastrous. In that second, at 60 mph, your car will travel 27 metres.

D 1

Using a mobile phone while you're driving is illegal. The chance of you having a collision while you are using one increases by four times. Be safe, switch it off and use the mail retrieval service. Wait until you're parked in a safe and proper place before you

- retrieve any messages
- make any calls
- send or receive texts.

"PEOPLE WHO RING YOU ON A MOBILE PHONE MAY NOT HAVE YOUR ROAD SAFETY AS A HIGH PRIORITY"

D 18

If you are driving on a motorway you should leave the motorway and stop in a safe place before using your phone.

If your vehicle has a navigation system, stop in a safe place before using the system.

FAQs

Is it OK to use a 'hands-free' phone when driving?

Just because it's hands-free doesn't make it safe, it can still distract you. The person you're talking to can't see the traffic situation. They won't stop speaking to you if you're approaching a hazard.

It's safer not to use a phone at all if you're driving. Wait and find a safe place to stop.

◄ HC
149

I've seen yellow lines painted at intervals across the road. What do they mean?

These encourage drivers to reduce their speed. They may be red. You often see them on approach to a

◄ D
6

◄ KYTS
68, 75

- *hazard (such as a roundabout)*
- *reduced speed limit.*

I have heard the term 'blind spot'. What does this mean?

Blind spots are areas that can't be seen either when using normal forward vision or when using the mirrors.

◄ HC
159

Be aware that a lorry driver can't see you if you're close behind. Keep well back so the driver can see you.

◄ D
4

"EXTERIOR MIRRORS WILL HELP REDUCE BLIND SPOTS"

2 Attitude

Safe driving is all about developing the correct attitude and approach together with a sound knowledge of driving techniques.

However good, fast or expensive your vehicle, it's you, the driver, who determines how safe it is.

Consideration

D 1

Be considerate to other road users. Other types of vehicle, cyclists and horse riders have just as much right to use the road as you. Don't drive in a competitive way, people who do this cause an increased risk for everyone on the road.

HC 214-215

Horses become frightened easily and the rider could lose control. When passing them

D 10

- keep your speed right down
- give them plenty of room.

Take care if there are animals, such as sheep, on the road. Stop and switch off your engine if necessary or if you're asked to do so.

HC 169

If you're driving a slow-moving vehicle, consider the other drivers behind you. If there's a long queue

D 10

- pull over as soon as you can do so safely
- let the traffic pass.

Try to be considerate. Think how you would feel if you were one of the following drivers. They may not be as patient as you are.

Help other road users by signalling correctly and taking up the correct position at junctions. For instance, if you want to turn right, get into the right-hand lane. A badly positioned vehicle could prevent following vehicles proceeding.

◀ HC 143

◀ D 7 + 8

Following safely

Keep a safe distance from the vehicle in front

- in good, dry conditions leave a two-second gap
- in wet weather leave four seconds.

Tailgating – driving too close to the vehicle in front – is

- very dangerous
- intimidating for the driver in front.

◀ HC 126

◀ D 7, 10 + 11

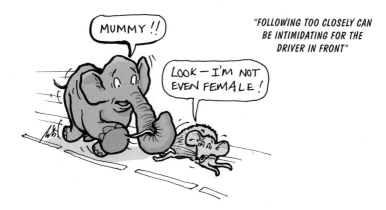

"FOLLOWING TOO CLOSELY CAN BE INTIMIDATING FOR THE DRIVER IN FRONT"

Keep well back, especially from a large vehicle. You'll be able to see further down the road and therefore be prepared for any hazards.

If the driver behind is following too closely, gradually increase the gap between you and the vehicle in front. This will give you a greater safety margin.

If another driver cuts in front of you, drop back to maintain your correct separation distance.

◀ D 7 + 10

◀ HC 168

Courtesy

HC 147 ▶

D 8 ▶

HC 112 ▶

D 3, 5 +10 ▶

Be patient with other road users. Be aware that not everyone obeys the rules. Try to be calm and tolerant, however difficult it seems. For instance, if a vehicle pulls out in front of you at a junction, slow down, don't get annoyed with them.

Only sound your horn if there's danger and you need to let others know you're there. Don't sound it through impatience.

"BE COURTEOUS AND DIP YOUR LIGHTS AT NIGHT TO AVOID DAZZLING OTHER DRIVERS"

HC 115 ▶

D 13 ▶

At night, don't dazzle other drivers. Dip your lights when you're

- following another vehicle
- meeting another vehicle.

If you're queuing in traffic at night, use your handbrake. Keeping your foot on the brake could dazzle the drivers behind you.

Priority

HC 219 ▶

D 7 ▶

Give priority to emergency vehicles. It's important for them to proceed quickly through traffic. Someone's life might depend on it. Pull over to let them through as soon as you can do so safely.

As well as the normal fire, police and ambulance, the following services may use a blue flashing light:

- coastguard
- bomb disposal
- mountain rescue
- blood transfusion.

Doctors may use green flashing lights.

Give priority to buses pulling out from bus stops, as long as you can do so safely. In some areas, bus lanes allow buses to proceed quickly through traffic. Be aware of road signs and markings so you don't use bus lanes while they're in operation.

HC
223
D
6, 7 + 10

At unmarked crossroads no-one has priority. Slow down and look both ways before pulling out.

Watch out for pedestrians at or approaching a zebra crossing:

HC
195
D
7

- be prepared to slow down and stop
- be patient if they're a bit slow
- don't encourage them to cross by waving or flashing your headlights – there may be another vehicle coming.

If you're approaching a pelican crossing and the amber light is flashing

HC
196-198
D
7

- give way to pedestrians on the crossing
- don't move off until the crossing is clear.

"PUFFIN CROSSINGS ARE
ELECTRONICALLY CONTROLLED"

Puffin crossings are electronically controlled. Sensors mean the red light stays on until the person has reached a safe position. There's no flashing amber phase – the sequence follows normal traffic lights.

HC
199
D
7
KYTS
124

Toucan crossings allow cyclists to cross at the same time as pedestrians.

FAQs

HC
300-306

D
7

KYTS
31

I've seen this sign – what does it mean?

This sign applies to trams only. Even if there aren't any trams where you live, you still need to know how to deal with them in case you ever visit a town which has them.

Give cyclists extra room where there are tram rails. The slippery rails may be difficult for them to negotiate.

HC
221

D
10

Why do large vehicles 'hog' the road?

Larger vehicles need more room to manoeuvre. This will affect their position when approaching junctions, especially when turning left. Keep well back and don't try to pass them on the left as the rear of the vehicle will cut in.

HC
168

D
7

A large vehicle is trying to overtake me, but is taking a long time, what should I do?

Slow down and let them pass. They will need more time than a car to pass you.

HC
168

D
7 + 11

What do I do if I'm travelling at the speed limit and a driver comes up behind flashing their headlights or trying to overtake?

Keep a steady course and allow them to overtake. Don't try to stop them, they could become more frustrated.

HC
110-111

D
5 + 10

I'm never too sure when I should flash my headlights.

Only flash your headlights to show other road users you're there. It's not a signal to show priority or impatience, nor to greet others.

16

3 Safety and your vehicle

Look after your car and it will look after you by being more economical and lasting longer. Remember that a clean engine is kinder to the environment.

"A CLEAN ENGINE IS KINDER TO THE ENVIRONMENT"

Basic maintenance

Regular care should ensure that your car is safe. Check

- lights, brakes, steering, exhaust system, seat belts, horn, speedometer, wipers and washers. These must all be working properly
- oil and water levels. This is especially important before a long journey (be careful not to overfill with oil as this can cause oil leaks)
- brake fluid. If this is allowed to get low it's dangerous and could cause an accident
- battery levels. Unless it is a maintenance-free battery, it may need topping up with distilled water
- the windscreen. This must be in good condition
- tyre pressures. Do this regularly, at least once a week. Check when they are cold to get a more accurate reading. Under-inflated tyres can affect
    - steering – it will feel heavy
    - fuel consumption – it may increase
    - braking

HC
p128-130

D
12 + 14

D
14

HC
p129

D
12 + 14

- tyre condition. The tread (on car and trailer tyres) must be at least 1.6 mm deep across the centre three-quarters of the breadth of the tyre and around the entire outer circumference. It's illegal to drive with tyres that have deep cuts in the side walls.

Uneven wear on the tyres can be caused by faults in the

- braking system
- suspension
- wheel alignment.

If the wheels are unbalanced they could cause the steering to vibrate.

Defects

If you've a basic understanding of how your car works it'll help you recognise the signs of a defect. It's important that your car's checked regularly by a qualified mechanic, especially the brakes and the steering.

Warning lights on the dashboard monitor the performance of the engine and give you warning of any defects.

- Check your vehicle handbook for their meaning.
- Don't ignore the warning – it could affect your safety.

The ABS warning light should go out when the vehicle's travelling at 5-10 mph. If it doesn't, have it checked by a qualified mechanic.

"TO CHECK THE SHOCK ABSORBERS 'BOUNCE' THE VEHICLE. IT SHOULDN'T CONTINUE TO BOUNCE UNDULY WHEN RELEASED"

18

To check the condition of the shock absorbers, 'bounce' the vehicle. Push down hard on each corner and it shouldn't continue to bounce unduly when released.

HC p130
D 14
D 14

Consult a garage as soon as possible if

- the steering vibrates – the wheels may need balancing
- the vehicle pulls to one side when you brake – your brakes may need adjusting.

Safety equipment

Modern cars are fitted with equipment designed with your safety in mind.

"YOU, AS A DRIVER, ARE RESPONSIBLE FOR MAKING SURE THAT CHILDREN UNDER 14 WEAR A SUITABLE RESTRAINT"

Wear your seat belt and make sure your passengers wear theirs (unless exempt). You, as a driver, are responsible for making sure that children under 14 wear a suitable restraint. If a correct child restraint is not available in the rear seat, an adult seat belt MUST be used. Never fit a rear-facing baby seat in a seat protected by an airbag. This could cause fatal injuries. The airbag MUST be deactivated first.

HC 99-102
D 2

When you get into the car

HC 97
D 3

D 4

- adjust the seat to ensure you can reach all the controls in comfort
- adjust the head restraint to help prevent neck injury in a collision
- wear suitable shoes so that you can keep control of the pedals
- adjust the mirrors to maximise your field of vision. Convex mirrors give a wider view but can make vehicles look further away than they are. If you're reversing and can't see behind you, get someone to guide you.

If visibility's poor, use dipped headlights. It's important for other road users to see you. If there's thick fog, use your fog lights.

HC 113-115, 226
D 12

When leaving your car on a two-way road at night, park in the direction of the traffic. If the speed limit is over 30 mph, switch on your parking lights.

Hazard warning lights are fitted so you can warn drivers of a hazard ahead, such as

- when you've broken down
- queuing traffic on a dual carriageway or motorway.

Don't use them as an excuse to park illegally, even for a short time.

Security

Make it as difficult as you can for a thief to either break into your car or steal it:

- engage the steering lock
- remove the keys and lock your car even if you're only leaving it for a short time
- lock any contents, especially valuables, out of sight, or better still take them with you
- don't leave the vehicle registration documents in the car. The thief could declare ownership
- at night, park in a well-lit area.

"YOU CAN FIT A VARIETY OF SECURITY DEVICES TO YOUR VEHICLE"

To make it more difficult for the opportunist thief you can

- fit an anti-theft alarm or immobiliser
- use a visible security device such as a steering wheel or handbrake lock
- have the vehicle registration number etched on the windows.

"CONSIDER JOINING A VEHICLE WATCH SCHEME IF THERE'S ONE IN YOUR AREA"

Radios and other forms of in-car entertainment are prime targets for thieves. If you can, install a security coded radio. This would be of little use if it was stolen.

Consider joining a vehicle watch scheme if there's one in your area.

Considering other road users

Avoid parking your vehicle where it would cause an obstruction to other road users, such as

◀ HC 243

- in front of a property entrance
- at or near a bus stop
- near the brow of a hill
- at a dropped kerb.

Never stop or park on or near a level crossing, or on the zigzag lines at a pedestrian crossing . This would block the view of pedestrians and drivers and endanger people trying to use the crossing.

◀ HC 240, 291

Environment

D 17 ►

Motor vehicles can harm the environment, resulting in

- air pollution
- damage to buildings
- using up of natural resources.

D 17 ►

Road transport accounts for 20% of all emissions. Help the environment by driving in an Eco-safe manner, you will improve road safety, reduce exhaust emissions and improve your fuel consumption. You should

- reduce your speed - vehicles travelling at 70mph use up to 30% more fuel than those travelling at 50mph
- plan well ahead so that you can drive smoothly - avoiding rapid acceleration and heavy braking can cut your fuel bill by up to 15%
- use selective gear changing - miss out some gears - this can help by reducing the amount of time you are accelerating, the time when your vehicle uses most fuel
- have your vehicle serviced and tuned properly
- make sure your tyres are correctly inflated
- avoid using leaded fuel.

Don't

D 17 ►

- carry unnecessary weight or leave an empty roof rack on your car
- over-rev in lower gears.
- leave the engine running unnecessarily - if your vehicle is stationary and likely to remain so for some time, switch off the engine.

Never leave your vehicle unattended with the engine running. Always switch off the engine and secure the vehicle before leaving it.

"MODERN TRAMS USE ELECTRIC POWER AND REDUCE TRAFFIC"

Try not to use your car to make a lot of short journeys, think about walking or cycling instead. Using public transport or sharing a car can reduce the volume of traffic and the emissions it creates.

D 17

Modern trams use electric power. They reduce traffic and noise pollution.

HC p130

Make sure your filler cap is securely fastened. If it's loose, it could spill fuel which wastes fuel and money. Spilt diesel fuel makes the road slippery for other road users.

D 14

"ENSURE THAT YOU TAKE YOUR CAR FOR REGULAR SERVICES"

Having your car serviced regularly will give better fuel economy and your exhaust emissions will be cleaner. If your vehicle is over three years old (over four years old in Northern Ireland), it will have to pass an emissions test as part of the MOT test.

D 17

If you service your own vehicle, dispose of old engine oil and batteries responsibly. Take them to a local authority site or a garage. Don't pour oil down the drain.

D 17

Also bear in mind noise pollution. In built-up areas don't use your car horn between 11.30 pm and 7.00 am, unless another vehicle poses a danger.

HC 112

D 3

Avoiding congestion

You will have an easier and more pleasant journey, if you

D
18 ▶

- plan your route before starting out
- avoid busy times, if possible
- allow plenty of time for your journey, especially if you have an appointment to keep or a connection to make.

Plan your route by

- looking at a map
- checking with a motoring organisation
- using a route planner on the internet.

If you are travelling on a new or unfamiliar route, it is a good idea to print out or write down the route, and also to plan an alternative route in case your original route is blocked.

If you can avoid travelling at busy times, you will

- be less likely to be delayed
- help to ease congestion for those who have to travel at these times.

D
18 ▶

In some areas those using congested road space have to pay a congestion charge. In London, those exempt from paying include

- disabled people who hold a Blue Badge
- riders of two-wheeled vehicles
- people living within the area.

FAQs

D
3 ▶

I have heard the term 'dry steering' – what does this mean?

This is when you turn the steering wheel while the car isn't moving. It can cause unnecessary wear to the tyres and steering mechanism.

What is a catalytic converter?

D
17 ▶

A catalytic converter is fitted to the exhaust and reduces emissions. It acts like a filter, removing some of the toxic waste.

Road humps have been installed in our area. What other types of traffic calming are there?

HC 153
D 6

As well as road humps, road narrowing and chicanes may be used. These are used to slow the traffic down, so keep your speed down throughout the area.

A reduced speed limit of 20 mph is being introduced into many narrow residential streets. Look out for the signs, and remember the measures are there for a good reason; they could save lives.

In an automatic car, what is 'kick down'?

D 22

This is a device that gives quick acceleration when needed, for example, to overtake. Excessive use of this will burn more fuel.

On a trip to London I saw red lines on the side of the road. What are they for?

HC p115
D 6

These indicate 'red routes'. They help the traffic flow by restricting stopping on these routes.

I've heard of 'brake fade'. What does it mean?

D 7

This is when the brakes become less effective because of overheating. It may happen if they're used continuously, such as on a long, steep downhill stretch of road. Using a lower gear will help braking.

HEY, LIKE, PEACE, MAN!

TEA + SCONES

"THERE ARE VARIOUS TYPES OF TRAFFIC CALMING SCHEMES"

4 Safety margins

It's essential that you always keep in mind the safety of not only yourself, but your passengers and other road users as well.

Reduce your chances of having an accident by knowing safety margins and the risk of not adhering to them. Never take unnecessary risks.

HC
160

D
5 + 7

Keep control of your car by using the correct procedures. For instance, when you're travelling downhill, control your speed by

- selecting a lower gear
- braking gently.

HC
122

Don't 'coast' (i.e. travel in neutral or with the clutch pressed down) as this reduces your control.

"COASTING IS DANGEROUS AS IT REDUCES YOUR CONTROL"

Stopping distance

HC
126

D
7

Leave enough room between you and the car in front so you can pull up safely if it slows down or stops suddenly. Your overall stopping distance is the distance your car travels

- from the moment you realise you must brake
- to the moment the vehicle stops.

This is made up of thinking distance and braking distance.

Study the typical thinking, braking and stopping distances given in *The Highway Code*. The figures given are the stopping distances if you're travelling in a vehicle with good tyres and brakes

- on a dry road
- in good conditions.

HC
202, 205

D
12

Don't just learn the figures – you need to be able to judge the distance. A useful method is to leave a two-second time gap between yourself and the vehicle in front.

In other conditions you need to increase these distances:

- when it's raining or the road is wet – double the distance
- when it's icy – ten times the distance.

In faster conditions such as on motorways, increasing the distance between vehicles helps to lower the risk of collision.

"IF THE WEATHER'S REALLY BAD, MAKE ALTERNATIVE ARRANGEMENTS"

Weather conditions

Weather conditions have a great effect on your safety margins. If the weather's really bad, such as snow, ice or thick fog, consider whether your journey's really necessary. Never underestimate the dangers.

HC
228-231

Before starting a journey in freezing weather, clear ice and snow from your windows, lights, mirrors and number plates.

D
12

When driving

- use the highest gear you can
- brake gently and in plenty of time
- be prepared to stop and clean your windscreen by hand if the wipers aren't effective.

When it's foggy

- allow more time for your journey
- slow down as your visibility is reduced
- increase the gap between your vehicle and the one in front of you
- use dipped headlights even in daylight. If visibility falls below 100 metres (328 feet) use fog lights if you've got them. Remember to switch them off when the fog lifts.

Aquaplaning may happen in heavy rain. The tyres lift off the road surface and skate on a film of water. The steering becomes light. If this happens

- ease off the accelerator
- don't brake until your steering feels normal again.

If you've driven through deep water such as a ford or a flood, test your brakes. If necessary, dry them out by pressing lightly on the brake pedal as you go along.

HC
234-236

D
12

HC
227

D
12

HC
121

D
12

"AQUAPLANING CAN OCCUR WHEN THE TYRES LIFT FROM THE ROAD SURFACE ON A FILM OF WATER"

Hot weather can also pose a danger. The road surface could become soft and your tyres might not grip so well. This may affect your

- braking
- steering.

HC 237
D 12

Bright sunlight can dazzle. Other drivers might not be able to see your indicators blinking if they are dazzled. Consider giving an arm signal as well.

High winds can blow you off course, especially on an open stretch of road. They have an even greater effect on high-sided vehicles, motorcyclists and cyclists. Take care if you pass these road users as they may be blown off course by a sudden gust. Allow extra room and then check your left side as you pass them.

HC 232-233
D 12

"BEWARE OF HIGH WINDS; CYCLISTS MAY BE BLOWN OFF COURSE BY A SUDDEN GUST"

Skidding

HC 119, 231
D 5 + 12

Skidding is mainly caused by the driver. Drivers need to adjust their driving to the road, weather and traffic conditions.

There's most risk of skidding in wet or icy conditions. Black ice isn't obvious until you feel the steering becoming light. Be aware that in very cold weather it could be a hazard.

Reduce the risk of skidding and wheelspin by driving

- at a low speed
- in as high a gear as possible.

HC
119, 231 ▶

D
5 ▶

Scan the road ahead for clues such as road signs and markings. You shouldn't then be taken by surprise. You can

- slow down gradually before you reach the hazard, such as a bend
- avoid sudden steering movements.

D
5 ▶

If you do start skidding

- release the footbrake and reapply it gently
- steer smoothly in the direction of the skid – if the back of the car skids to the right, steer carefully to the right, and vice versa.

HC
120 ▶

D
3 + 5 ▶

Anti-lock braking systems (ABS) reduce the risk of skidding if you have to brake in an emergency. Wheel speed sensors anticipate when a wheel is about to lock. If you're driving a vehicle with ABS

- apply the footbrake rapidly and firmly
- don't release the brake pedal until you have stopped.

ABS doesn't necessarily reduce your stopping distance but you can continue to steer while braking because the wheels are prevented from locking. It may not work as effectively where there's

- surface water
- a loose road surface.

Contraflow systems

Where a temporary contraflow system is in operation, you will be travelling close to oncoming traffic, sometimes in narrow lanes. When you enter a contraflow system you should

HC
160 ▶

D
7 ▶

- reduce speed in good time
- choose an appropriate lane in good time
- keep the correct separation distance.

FAQs

HC
252

D
9

Why does my instructor tell me to keep well to the left before a right-hand bend?

Keeping well to the left improves your view of the road ahead and gives you an earlier indication of any hazards.

"WHEN OVERTAKING, ALWAYS ENSURE YOU'VE ENOUGH TiME TO COMPLETE THE MANOEUVRE SAFELY"

How can I park my car safely on a downhill slope?

Apply the handbrake firmly and turn the steering wheel towards the kerb. This will help stop your vehicle rolling downhill.

HC
163-167

D
7

I know overtaking is a dangerous manoeuvre – are there any places that I definitely need to avoid?

Always ensure you've enough time to complete the manoeuvre safely. In particular don't overtake

- *where your view ahead is blocked (e.g. by a bend)*
- *when approaching a junction*
- *if you're intending to turn off the road shortly afterwards.*

D
22

What are the benefits of a four-wheel drive vehicle?

It has improved road holding. The extra grip helps when travelling on slippery or uneven roads.

HC
153

D
6

Why are there so many speed humps around?

These traffic calming measures are normally found in built-up areas to improve the safety of the area. Slow right down as you approach and drive over them.

5 Hazard awareness

When you start to learn to drive you'll be concentrating on the basic controls of the car. As your skill improves so will your ability to recognise hazards on the road.

A hazard is a situation which may require you as a driver to respond by taking action such as braking or steering.

"WHEN YOU START TO LEARN TO DRIVE YOU'LL BE CONCENTRATING ON THE BASIC CONTROLS OF THE CAR"

These can be

- static hazards – such as roundabouts and junctions
- moving hazards – other road users
- road and weather conditions.

Static hazards

There are numerous types of static hazard, including bends, junctions, roundabouts, parked vehicles and skips in the road, roadworks, traffic calming, different types of crossings and traffic lights.

D
10

HC
153

D
7, 8 + 10

All of these may require you to respond in some way, so

- take a mental note of their existence
- slow down and get ready to stop if necessary.

Road signs and markings are there to give you clues. Learn their meanings. Watch out for them so that you can reduce your speed in good time and prepare yourself for any action you may need to take. The same applies to traffic lights, other light signals and signals from police officers.

HC
102-117

D
6

KYTS
10-71 +
77-93

If you see a sign for a bend ask yourself, 'What if there was a pedestrian or obstruction just around the bend, could I stop in time? Could I do it safely?'

In busy areas, parked cars can cause a hazard, especially if parked illegally, for example on the zigzag lines by a pedestrian crossing. Watch out for

HC
205-206

D
7 + 10

- children dashing out from between the cars
- car doors opening
- cars moving away.

Would you be able to stop?

There's often reduced visibility at junctions, especially in built-up areas. Take extra care and pull forward slowly until you can see down the road. You may also be able to see reflections of traffic in shop windows.

HC
151

D
10

Don't block a junction, leave it clear to allow vehicles to enter and emerge.

Where lanes are closed be ready for cars cutting in front of you and keep a safe distance from the vehicle in front.

D
8 + 11

If you are driving on a motorway or dual carriageway and see a hazard or obstruction ahead, briefly use your hazard warning lights to warn the traffic behind.

HC
116

If your vehicle has broken down and is causing an obstruction, switch on your hazard warning lights to warn other road users.

Moving hazards

You need to look out for other types of road user; pedestrians, cyclists, horse riders, large vehicle drivers, motorcyclists, disabled people using a powered vehicle and other car drivers.

"GIVE CYCLISTS
PLENTY OF ROOM;
THEY MAY HAVE TO
WOBBLE OR SWERVE TO
AVOID POTHOLES"

In built-up areas you may come across pedestrians in the road; be patient and wait for them to finish crossing.

On country roads, there may be no pavement, so look out for pedestrians in the road. They may be walking towards you on your side of the road.

Be aware of cyclists and give them plenty of room:

- they may wobble or swerve to avoid drains or potholes
- at junctions or traffic lights, give them time to turn or pull away
- before you turn left, check for cyclists filtering on your left.

If you see a bus at a bus stop, think

- people may get off the bus and move across the road
- the bus may be about to move off.

School buses might stop at places other than bus stops.

At some bridges, high vehicles may need to use the centre of the road to be able to pass underneath.

Watch out for other vehicles, especially motorcyclists, overtaking and cutting in front of you. If you need to, drop back to retain a safe separation distance.

HC
211-214

D
10

HC
223

D
10

HC
168

Elderly drivers may not react very quickly, so be patient with them.

HC
216

Some vehicles have signs on the back, for example those with arrows, large goods vehicles over 13 metres long and vehicles carrying hazardous chemicals. Learn what they mean.

HC
p117

Yourself

Don't allow yourself to become a hazard on the road. You need to be alert at all times.

Make sure you use your mirrors so you are aware of what is going on around you at all times. These may be convex to give a wider field of vision.

HC
161

Don't drive if you're tired. Plan your journey so that you've enough rest and refreshment breaks. Try to stop at least once every two hours. Always make sure you've plenty of fresh air in your car, by opening a window.

HC
91

D
1 + 11

If you feel tired

- pull over at a safe and legal place to rest
- on a motorway, leave at the next exit or services.

Your concentration can also be affected by

HC
148-150

- using a mobile phone
- loud music
- looking at a map.

D
1

D
1

If you've had an argument, calm down before starting or continuing your journey.

Never drive if you've been drinking. It's not worth taking a chance. If you're driving, don't drink alcohol. If you've had a drink, go home by public transport.

HC
95

D
1

Alcohol

- reduces concentration, coordination and control
- gives a false sense of confidence
- reduces your judgement of speed
- slows down your reactions.

You must be fit to drive. Certain medicines can make you drowsy; check the label or ask your doctor or pharmacist if it's safe for you to drive after taking medication that may affect your driving.

HC
90, 96

**"IF YOU NEED GLASSES TO DRIVE,
WEAR THEM EVERY TIME YOU DRIVE"**

D
1

Using illegal drugs is highly dangerous and the effects of some can last up to 72 hours. Never take them before driving. If you've been convicted of driving whilst unfit through drink or drugs, the cost of your insurance will rise considerably.

HC
90, 92-94

D
1

Your eyesight should be of a safe standard.If you need glasses to drive, wear them every time you drive. If you can't find them, don't drive. Don't wear tinted glasses at night.

You must tell the licensing authority if

• your eyesight deteriorates
• you suffer from an illness which may affect your driving.

Road and weather conditions

Different types of weather can change a normal stretch of road into a hazard. Rain, ice, fog and even bright sunlight can have an effect on safety. Drive accordingly and be aware of the added dangers.

HC
227

D
12

In wet weather

• double your separation distance to four seconds
• spray may reduce your vision.

FAQs

How do I deal with inconsiderate drivers?

There are occasions when we all make misjudgements or mistakes. Be aware that other drivers might not always follow the rules. Stay calm. Don't shout or make rude gestures, this won't help the situation at all.

HC
146-147

D
1 + 3

- *Wait if necessary to allow the other driver to move out of the way.*
- *If you feel upset, stop and take a break if you can.*

Good anticipation skills can help to prevent these incidents becoming accidents.

What restrictions are there on provisional licence holders?

HC
253, p123

You must not drive

- *on your own*
- *on a motorway.*

"GOOD ANTICIPATION SKILLS CAN HELP PREVENT INCIDENTS BECOMING ACCIDENTS"

Are there any moving picture questions in the theory test?

Yes, the hazard perception part of the theory test consists of a series of video clips. The training material for this, called RoadSense, is available as a video and workbook or in DVD format.

D
10 ▶

How do you prevent the car behind driving too closely?

Move over and let the car through if you can. If there's no room and the driver behind seems to be 'pushing' you, increase your distance from the car in front. This will lessen the risk of an accident involving several vehicles.

"HOW DO YOU PREVENT THE VEHICLE BEHIND FROM FOLLOWING TOO CLOSELY?"

HC
110, 112 ▶
D
5 ▶

What do I do if a car is about to reverse out in front of me?

Reduce your speed and be prepared to stop. Sound your horn to warn them you're there (in built-up areas between 11.30 pm and 7 am, flash your headlights instead).

What do I do if I take the wrong route and find myself in a one-way street?

Don't try to turn round in a one-way street. Continue to the end of the road and then find a safe place to turn round.

"IF THE DRIVER IN FRONT HAS
FORGOTTEN TO CANCEL THEIR RIGHT
INDICATOR, BE CAUTIOUS, STAY BEHIND
AND DON'T OVERTAKE"

What do I do if it looks like the driver in front has forgotten to cancel their right indicator?

Be cautious. Stay behind and don't overtake – they may be unsure of the position of a junction and turn suddenly.

What is 'kick-down'?

If you're driving a car with automatic transmission and you need quick acceleration, sharply pressing the accelerator pedal right down causes a quick change down to the next lower gear. This is known as 'kick-down'.

6 Vulnerable road users

The most vulnerable road users are pedestrians, cyclists, motorcyclists and horse riders. Always be aware of their presence and treat them with respect. It's particularly important to show consideration to children, elderly and disabled people.

Learners, inexperienced and older drivers are the most vulnerable types of driver.

Pedestrians

HC
2, 206 ▶

Pedestrians normally use a pavement or footpath. Take extra care if they have to walk in the road

D
10 ▶

- when the pavement is closed due to street repairs
- on country roads where there's no pavement.

"WATCH OUT FOR PEDESTRIANS ALREADY CROSSING WHEN YOU'RE TURNING INTO A SIDE ROAD"

KYTS
13 ▶

On country roads, pedestrians are advised to walk on the right-hand side of the road so they are facing oncoming traffic. Signs may warn you of people walking in the road.

HC
5 ▶

A large group of people, such as those on an organised walk, may walk on the left-hand side. At night the person at the rear should carry a bright red light to warn approaching vehicles of their presence.

Watch out for pedestrians already crossing when you're turning into a side road. They have priority, so wait for them to cross.

HC
170
D
8

Be ready to slow down and stop as you approach a pedestrian crossing.

HC
195-199
D
7

- Zebra crossings – slow down and prepare to stop if someone is waiting to cross
- Pelican crossings are light controlled. During the flashing amber phase, give way to pedestrians on the crossing. If the lights change to green while someone is still crossing, be patient and wait until they have finished crossing.
- Puffin crossings have sensors to detect when people are on the crossing. The lights don't change from red until the crossing is clear.
- Toucan crossings – cyclists can cross at the same time as pedestrians. There's no flashing amber phase.

Children

Children cause particular problems because they can be unpredictable. They are less likely than other pedestrians to look before stepping into the road.

HC
208-210
D
10

"CHILDREN POSE PARTICULAR PROBLEMS BECAUSE THEY CAN BE UNPREDICTABLE"

Drive carefully near schools:

- there may be flashing amber lights under a school warning sign. Reduce your speed until you're clear of the area
- be prepared for a school crossing patrol to stop the traffic by stepping out into the road with a stop sign.

HC
208, 238

D
6

KYTS
56

HC
209, 117

Don't wait or park on yellow zigzag lines outside a school. A clear view of the crossing area outside the school is needed by

- drivers on the road
- pedestrians on the pavement.

Buses and coaches carrying schoolchildren show a special sign in the back. This indicates that they may stop frequently and not just at normal bus stops.

Elderly and disabled pedestrians

HC
207

D
10

If you see elderly people about to cross the road ahead, be careful, as they may have misjudged your speed.

If they are crossing, be patient and allow them to cross in their own time.

Treat disabled pedestrians as you would able-bodied, but be patient as they may need extra time to cross the road.

"IF ELDERLY PEDESTRIANS ARE CROSSING, BE PATIENT AND ALLOW THEM TO CROSS IN THEIR OWN TIME"

A pedestrian with hearing difficulties may have a dog with a

- distinctive yellow or burgundy coloured coat or
- distinctive orange lead and collar.

Take extra care as they may not be aware of vehicles approaching.

A person carrying a white stick with a red band is both deaf and blind.

Cyclists

Cyclists should normally follow the same rules as drivers, but they are slower and more vulnerable. In some areas signs may indicate special cycle or shared cycle and pedestrian routes.

Advanced stop lines are provided to allow cyclists to position themselves in front of other traffic. When the lights are red or about to become red you should stop at the first white line.

If you're overtaking a cyclist, give them as much room as you would a car. They may need to swerve

- to avoid an uneven road surface
- if they're affected by the wind.

A cyclist going slowly, or glancing over their shoulder to check for traffic, may be planning to turn right. Stay behind and give them plenty of room.

Never overtake a cyclist (or moped) just before you turn left. Hold back and wait until they have passed the junction before you turn.

When you're emerging from a junction, look carefully for cyclists. They're not as easy to see as larger vehicles. Also look out for cyclists emerging from junctions.

Be aware of cyclists at a roundabout. They are slower and more vulnerable than other road users, and may decide to stay in the left-hand lane whatever direction they're planning to take. Hold back and give them plenty of room.

Motorcyclists

Several of the points above are also relevant to motorcyclists. Remember to leave extra room while following or overtaking a motorcycle, and look out for indications that they may be about to turn right. Look carefully for them at junctions, as they are smaller than other road users and are harder to see.

When you're moving in queues of traffic be aware that motorcyclists may

- filter between lanes
- cut in just in front of you
- pass very close to you.

"WHEN YOU'RE MOVING IN QUEUES OF TRAFFIC BE AWARE THAT MOTORCYCLISTS MAY FILTER BETWEEN LANES"

HC
180 ▶

Before you turn right, always check for other traffic, especially motorcyclists, who may be overtaking.

If there's a slow-moving motorcyclist ahead and you're unsure what the rider is going to do, stay behind them in case they need to change direction suddenly.

HC
86 ▶

In order to improve their visibility, motorcyclists often wear bright clothing and ride with dipped headlights, even during the day.

HC
283 ▶
D
16 ▶

Motorcyclists also wear safety equipment, such as a helmet, to protect themselves. If there's been an accident and you find a motorcyclist has been injured, seek medical assistance. Don't remove their helmet unless it's essential.

Animals

HC
214-215 ▶
D
10 ▶

Always drive carefully if there are horses or other animals on the road. Go very slowly and be ready to stop.

When it's safe to overtake

- drive slowly
- leave plenty of room.

Take particular care when approaching a roundabout. Horse riders, like cyclists, may keep to the left, even if they're signalling right. Stay well back.

◄
HC
187

◄ D
8

Other drivers

The reactions of other drivers, especially inexperienced or older drivers, may be slower than yours. Learner drivers may make a mistake such as stalling at a junction. Try to be patient.

◄ HC
216-217

◄ D
1

Statistics show that 17 to 25 year olds are the most likely to be involved in a road accident. Newly qualified drivers can decrease their risk of accidents, particularly on the motorway, by taking further training. Find out more about the *Pass Plus* scheme from your ADI or by calling **0115 901 2633** (Pass Plus is not available in Northern Ireland).

◄
D
11

◄
HC
p134

FAQs

Reversing seems to be a dangerous manoeuvre. How can I be sure it's safe?

◄ D
9

Always check the area behind the car very carefully. Look especially for children, who are difficult to see. Get out and check if you're not sure. Stop and give way to any pedestrians crossing the road behind you.

"LOOK ESPECIALLY FOR CHILDREN, WHO ARE DIFFICULT TO SEE"

What should I do if parked vehicles restrict my view when emerging from a junction?

Stop, then creep forward slowly until you've a clear view.

How can I tell if someone is going to cross the road between parked cars?

You can't, but look for tell-tale signs such as a ball bouncing out into the road or a bicycle wheel sticking out between cars. Slow down and be prepared to stop.

"LOOK FOR TELL-TALE SIGNS SUCH AS A BALL BOUNCING OUT ONTO THE ROAD"

Who is most vulnerable at road junctions?

Junctions are dangerous places, especially for those who can't be seen as easily, e.g. pedestrians, cyclists and motorcyclists. Always take extra care.

What does a flashing amber beacon on the top of a vehicle mean?

This indicates a slow-moving vehicle. A powered vehicle used by a disabled person must have a flashing amber light when travelling on a dual carriageway.

Why do I need to be careful if a bus has stopped on the other side of the road?

Pedestrians may come from behind the bus and cross the road, or dash across from your left.

If I have a collision, what's the first thing I have to do?

Stop. By law, you must stop at the scene of the accident if damage or injury is caused to any other person, vehicle, animal or property.

HC
286

D
16

A friend wants to teach me to drive. Do they need any special qualifications?

Anyone who accompanies you must

- *be over 21*
- *have held, and still hold, a full licence for that category of vehicle for at least three years.*

You're strongly advised to take lessons with an Approved Driving Instructor to ensure that you're taught the correct procedures from the start.

HC
123

D
1

What can I do if I'm being dazzled by the vehicle behind?

Set your mirror to anti-dazzle, if you're able. Slow down and stop if you can't see.

D
4

WOWEE !!

LO-COST LESSONS

"WHAT CAN I DO IF I AM BEING DAZZLED BY THE VEHICLE BEHIND?"

7 Other types of vehicle

You need to take extra care when meeting or following different types of vehicle, both smaller and larger vehicles.

Motorcycles

HC
232-233

D
12

Motorcyclists are affected more than other vehicles by windy weather. They can be blown sideways and veer into your path more easily, so

- if you're overtaking a motorcyclist allow extra room
- if a motorcyclist in front of you is overtaking a high-sided vehicle, keep well back as they could be blown off course.

HC
p109

Watch out for signs warning you that the road is particularly susceptible to side winds.

HC
213

D
10

Motorcyclists may swerve into the road to avoid uneven or slippery surfaces. Metal drain covers in wet weather are particularly hazardous for two-wheeled vehicles.

Large vehicles

HC
164, 222

D
7

Large vehicles reduce your view of the road ahead. Keep well back if you're following a large vehicle, especially if you're hoping to overtake. If another car fills the gap you've left, drop back further. This will improve your view of the road ahead.

HC
232-233

D
7 + 12

Overtaking a lorry is more risky because of the length of the vehicle - it takes longer to overtake. Never begin to overtake unless you're sure that you can complete the manoeuvre safely.

HC
227

D
11 + 12

In wet weather large vehicles throw up a lot of spray. This can affect your visibility so drop back further until you can see better. If the spray makes it difficult for you to be seen

- use dipped headlights
- use rear fog lights if visibility is seriously reduced, i.e. less than 100 metres (328 feet).

Stay well back and give lorries plenty of room as they approach or emerge from

- road junctions
- crossroads
- mini-roundabouts.

To get round a corner, they may need to move in the opposite direction to which they're indicating. This is because of the length of their vehicle. If they want to turn left, they may indicate left but move over to the right, and vice versa.

HC 221
D 8

If you're waiting to emerge left from a minor road and a large vehicle is approaching from the right, wait. It may seem as if there's time to turn but the large vehicle could easily hide an overtaking vehicle.

Buses

Bus drivers need to make frequent stops. If a bus pulls up at a bus stop, watch carefully for pedestrians who may get off and cross the road in front of or behind the bus.

D 8

Be prepared to give way to a bus which is trying to move off from a bus stop, as long as it's safe to do so.

Trams

HC 223
D 10

Trams operate in some cities. Take extra care – they

- are silent
- move quickly
- can't steer to avoid you.

In these cities, there may be additional white light signals at some traffic lights. These are especially for tram drivers.

HC 224
D 7

FAQs

What kind of rear view mirror should I use if I'm towing a caravan?

It's safest to use extended-arm side mirrors. These help you get a better view behind and around the caravan.

D 19

D
7

If I'm driving downhill and a lorry coming uphill needs to move out to pass a parked car, should I stop for it?

Slow down and give way if possible. It's much more difficult for large vehicles to stop and then start up again if they are going uphill.

D
12

Which vehicles are most affected by crosswinds?

Crosswinds are much more likely to affect cyclists, motorcyclists and high-sided vehicles than they are cars. If you're following or overtaking, be aware that they might swerve suddenly and allow extra room.

HC
135
D
7

Why are two-way roads divided into three lanes more dangerous?

Traffic in both directions can use the middle lane to overtake, so approaching traffic could be intending to make the same manoeuvre at the same time.

HC
36, 220

Is there a speed limit for powered vehicles used by disabled people?

Powered vehicles, such as wheelchairs and scooters, used by disabled people have a maximum speed limit of 8mph when used on the road.

8 Vehicle handling

Various conditions can affect the handling of your vehicle. These can roughly be divided into

- weather and light conditions
- control and speed
- road surfaces.

Weather conditions

HC
126, 227

D
12

Rain or wet conditions

When it's raining or the road is wet, leave at least double the normal stopping distance. If you're following a vehicle at a safe distance and another vehicle pulls into the gap you've left, drop back to regain a safe distance.

When visibility is poor but not seriously reduced during the day, use dipped headlights to help other road users to see you.

"THERE MAY BE A DEPTH GUAGE AT A FORD, THIS WILL HELP YOU DECIDE WHETHER YOU SHOULD GO THROUGH"

In winter a ford is more likely to flood, making it difficult to cross. There may be a depth gauge, which will help you decide whether you should go through. If you decide to continue

- use a low gear
- drive through slowly
- test your brakes afterwards: wet brakes are less effective.

Fog

When visibility is seriously reduced you must use headlights, or fog lights if you have them. 'Seriously reduced' generally means if you can't see for more than 100 metres (328 feet).

Never use front or rear fog lights unless visibility is seriously reduced. If you've been using them and conditions improve, remember to switch them off. Don't use fog lights when they're not needed because

- you may be breaking the law
- they can dazzle other drivers
- drivers behind you won't be able to see your brake lights as clearly, or they may think you're braking when you're not.

Always keep your speed down in foggy weather, as it's harder to see what is happening ahead. Increase your distance from the vehicle in front, in case it stops or slows suddenly.

Be especially careful when driving on motorways in fog: reflective studs help you to see the road ahead. In particular

- red studs mark the left-hand edge of the carriageway
- amber studs mark the central reservation.

Very bad weather

If it's very foggy or snow is falling heavily, don't travel unless your journey is essential. If you must travel, take great care and allow plenty of time.

Before you start out, make sure that

- your lights are working
- your windows are clean.

In deep snow, consider fitting chains to your wheels to help grip and prevent skidding.

IF SNOW IS FALLING HEAVILY, DON'T TRAVEL UNLESS YOUR JOURNEY IS ESSENTIAL. IF YOU MUST TRAVEL, TAKE GREAT CARE AND ALLOW PLENTY OF TIME."

When on the road keep well back – increase the gap between yourself and the vehicle ahead in case it stops suddenly. In icy conditions it can take ten times the normal distance to stop compared to dry conditions.

Windy weather

Wind can affect all vehicles. A sudden gust may catch your vehicle

- when passing a high-sided vehicle on the motorway
- when driving on an exposed stretch of road.

HC
232

D
11 + 12

Driving at night

Make sure that your headlights don't dazzle

- the vehicle you're following
- any oncoming traffic.

If you're dazzled by the headlights of an oncoming vehicle, slow down or stop to remain in full control.

HC
114-115

D
13

"IF YOU'RE DAZZLED BY THE HEADLIGHTS OF AN ONCOMING VEHICLE, SLOW DOWN OR STOP TO REMAIN IN FULL CONTROL"

Be extra careful when you overtake at night. You can't see as far ahead and there may be bends in the road.

On a motorway, use

- dipped headlights, even if the road is well-lit
- sidelights if you're broken down on the hard shoulder. This will help other road users to see you.

Control and speed

HC
122 ▶

D
5 + 7 ▶

D
11 + 15 ▶

Keep full control of your vehicle at all times. Driving with the clutch down or in neutral for any length of time (coasting) reduces control, especially of steering and braking. This is especially dangerous when travelling downhill as the vehicle will pick up speed quickly and there's no engine braking.

You can use your vehicle's engine to help control your speed. Select a lower gear when driving down a steep hill. This can be especially important as your brakes may become less effective due to overheating.

D
7 ▶

When driving up a steep hill, the engine will work harder and you'll slow down sooner.

Take extra care on a single-track road. If you see a vehicle coming towards you pull into, or opposite, a passing place.

Always drive in accordance with the conditions. Your stopping distance will be affected by

- your speed
- the condition of your tyres
- the weather.

Try to avoid skidding, as it can be hard to regain control once a skid has started. If you do not have anti-lock brakes and your vehicle begins to skid when you are braking on a wet road, the first thing you should do is release the footbrake. If the rear wheels of your vehicle begin to skid, steer into the skid by turning the steering wheel in the same direction. Avoid braking suddenly or harshly, as this will make the situation worse.

Traffic calming and road surfaces

Traffic calming is used to slow down traffic and make the roads safer for vulnerable road users, especially pedestrians. One of the most common measures is road humps (sometimes called speed humps). Stay within the speed limit and don't overtake other vehicles within these areas.

HC
155

D
10

D
7

D
5

HC
153

D
6

"ONE OF THE MOST COMMON
MEASURES IS SPEED HUMPS"

In towns where trams operate, the areas used by the trams may have a different surface texture or colour. This may be edged with white line markings.

"A RUMBLE DEVICE (RAISED MARKINGS ACROSS THE ROAD) IS OFTEN USED TO ALERT YOU TO A HAZARD"

A rumble device (raised markings across the road) is often used to

• alert you to a hazard, such as a roundabout
• encourage you to reduce speed.

FAQs

Am I allowed to wait in a box junction?

Yes, if you want to turn right and your exit's clear but you're prevented from turning by oncoming traffic.

Do I need to leave sidelights on when I park on a two-way road?

Leave your sidelights on

• *if the speed limit's more than 30 mph*
• *when it's foggy.*

Always park on the left hand side of the road.

I'm following a slow-moving vehicle. I want to overtake but it's been signalling right for some time. What should I do?

HC
167

Wait for the signal to be cancelled before overtaking. The other driver may have misjudged the distance to a road junction or there might be a hidden hazard.

Are there any times when I can overtake on the left?

HC
163

D
7

Yes

- *if you're in a one-way street*
- *when the vehicle in front is signalling to turn right*
- *in slow-moving queues when traffic in the right-hand lane is moving more slowly than traffic in your lane.*

9 Motorway rules

Motorways are designed to help traffic travel faster. Conditions can change more quickly than on other roads, so you need to be especially alert at all times.

Check your vehicle thoroughly before starting a long motorway journey. Continuous high speeds may increase the risk of your vehicle breaking down.

Driving on the motorway

To join the motorway

- use the slip road to adjust your speed to traffic already on the motorway
- always give way to traffic already on the motorway.

Once you've joined the motorway, keep in the left-hand lane while you get used to the higher speeds of motorway traffic.

All traffic should normally use the left-hand lane of the motorway unless overtaking, regardless of the speed they're travelling. Use the middle and right-hand lane only for overtaking other vehicles.

When you overtake

- normally only overtake on the right
- you may overtake on the left if traffic is moving slowly in queues and the queue on your right is moving more slowly than the one you're in.

Where there's a steep uphill gradient, a separate crawler lane may be provided for slow-moving vehicles. This helps the faster-moving traffic to flow more easily.

If you're travelling in the left-hand lane and traffic is joining from a slip road, move to another lane if you're able. This helps the flow of traffic joining the motorway, especially at peak times.

Countdown markers on the left-hand verge indicate that you're approaching the next exit. If you want to leave the motorway, try to get into the left-hand lane in good time. If, by mistake, you go past the exit you wanted, carry on to the next one. Never try to stop or reverse.

Speed limits

The national speed limit for cars and motorcycles on a motorway is 70 mph. The same limit applies to all lanes. Obey any signs showing a lower speed limit.

HC 261, p40

D 11

A vehicle towing a trailer

- is restricted to a lower speed limit of 60 mph
- is not allowed to travel in the right-hand lane of a three-lane motorway unless there are lane closures.

In Northern Ireland, a vehicle towing a trailer should not use the right-hand lane of a three-lane motorway.

You can use your hazard lights to show following traffic that the traffic ahead is slowing down or stopping suddenly. Switch them off as soon as a queue forms behind you.

HC 116

D 11

As you approach any roadworks, take extra care. There are usually lower speed limits, especially if there's a contraflow system.

HC 289-290

D 11

- Obey all speed limits.
- Keep a good distance from the vehicle ahead.

"REFLECTIVE STUDS HELP YOU TO IDENTIFY YOUR POSITION ON THE CARRIAGEWAY"

Congestion relief

D 18 ▶

A pilot scheme called Active Traffic Management (ATM) is being trialled on some motorways to help reduce congestion. Where this is operating, mandatory speed limit signs will show on the gantries. If traffic speed can stay constant over a longer distance, bunching will be reduced and journey times will normally improve.

HC 269 ▶

In ATM areas, the hard shoulder may be used as a running lane. You will know when you can use this because a speed limit sign will be shown above all lanes, including the hard shoulder. A red cross showing above the hard shoulder indicates that you shouldn't travel in this lane and it should be used only in an emergency or breakdown.

Emergency Refuge Areas have also been built in these areas for use in cases of emergency or breakdown.

D 18 ▶

In a further bid to reduce congestion, Highways Agency Traffic Officers are being introduced on motorways throughout England, they

- are able to stop and direct anyone on a motorway
- answer motorway emergency telephones which are linked to Highways Agency Control centres in some areas.

Lane markings

HC 132 ▶
D 11 ▶

Reflective studs help you to identify your position on the carriageway, especially at night or in fog. The different colours are as follows:

- red – between the hard shoulder and carriageway
- amber – between the edge of the carriageway and the central reservation
- white – between lanes
- green – between the carriageway and slip roads
- fluorescent green/yellow – at contraflow systems and roadworks.

Stopping and breakdowns

Only stop on the motorway

HC
258, 270

D
11

- if flashing red lights show above every lane
- when told to do so by the police
- in a traffic jam
- in an emergency or breakdown.

Move over if signals on the overhead gantries advise you to do so.

KYTS
90

Only stop on the hard shoulder in an emergency. To stop for any other reason, such as to have a rest or look at a map, either leave at the next exit or go to a service area.

HC
270

D
11

If your vehicle breaks down or has a puncture, try to get onto the hard shoulder and call for help. If you can, use one of the emergency telephones which are

HC
275

D
15

- normally at one mile intervals. Marker posts at 100 metre intervals point you in the direction of the nearest phone
- connected direct to police control. They will be able to locate you easily.

When using an emergency phone, stand and face oncoming traffic. You can then see any hazards approaching: for example, the draught from a large vehicle could unsteady you if you're taken unawares.

If you decide to use your mobile phone

- check your location (the number on the nearest marker post) before you make the call
- give this information to the emergency services.

To rejoin the carriageway from the hard shoulder, wait for a safe gap and then gain speed on hard shoulder before moving out onto the main carriageway.

HC
276

D
15

If you're not able to get onto the hard shoulder when you break down

HC
277

D
15

- switch on your hazard warning lights
- leave your vehicle only when you can get clear of the carriageway safely.

FAQs

HC
253

D
11

Can I drive on a motorway with a provisional car or motorcycle licence?

You can't drive or ride on the motorway until you've passed your test, but you can drive or ride on dual carriageways.

I know that pedestrians and horse riders can't use a motorway – what vehicles aren't allowed?

The following vehicles aren't allowed on a motorway:

- *bicycles*
- *motorcycles under 50 cc*
- *most invalid carriages*
- *agricultural vehicles*
- *certain slow-moving vehicles.*

"CAN I DRIVE ON A MOTORWAY WITH A PROVISIONAL CAR OR MOTORCYCLE LICENCE?"

10 Rules of the road

It's important that everyone knows and follows the rules of the road. Some are legal requirements and some are just recommended best practice, but all help to make the roads safer.

Speed limits

HC
124, p40

You must not exceed the speed limit for the road you're on or your vehicle. Where there isn't any other limit shown, the national speed limit for cars and motorcycles is

- 60 mph on a single carriageway road
- 70 mph on a dual carriageway or motorway.

DIDN'T I TELL YOU, KEVAN, THAT THERE WOULD BE TROUBLE IF YOU STRAPPED THAT AERO-ENGINE ON YOUR FATHER'S CAR?

"THE NATIONAL SPEED LIMIT FOR CARS IS 60 MPH ON A SINGLE CARRIAGEWAY ROAD AND 70 MPH ON A DUAL CARRIAGEWAY OR MOTORWAY"

HC
124, p40 ▶

Lower speed limits of

- 50 mph on a single carriageway road
- 60 mph on a dual carriageway or motorway

apply for vehicles towing a trailer or caravan.

Street lights normally mean that there's a 30 mph speed limit for all vehicles unless signs show otherwise.

HC
p107 ▶

On some roads you may also find a minimum speed limit where you should travel above the limit shown on the sign unless it's unsafe to do so.

HC
152 ▶
D
10 ▶

Always drive with care and according to the conditions. If you're going along a street where cars are parked, keep your speed down and beware of

- pedestrians (especially children) emerging from behind parked vehicles
- vehicles pulling out
- drivers' doors opening.

HC
288 ▶
KYTS ▶
89

At roadworks there may be temporary speed limits to slow traffic down. Always obey these signs.

Lanes and junctions

HC
140-141 ▶
KYTS ▶
30

Some roads have lanes reserved for specific vehicles such as cycles, buses or trams. These are marked by signs and road markings, and must only be used by those vehicles during their hours of operation.

Never drive or park in a cycle lane marked by a solid white line during its period of operation. Don't drive or park in one marked by a broken line unless it's unavoidable.

HC
145 ▶

Only drive over a footpath to gain access to a property.

On a dual carriageway, the right-hand lane is only for turning right or overtaking. The same rule applies to three-lane dual carriageways.

HC
181-183 ▶
D
8 ▶

Treat junctions with extra care. On approach, move into the appropriate position in good time. If you're going to turn left, keep well to the left as you approach the junction.

"ONLY DRIVE OVER A FOOTPATH TO GAIN ACCESS TO A PROPERTY"

If you're turning right at a crossroads when an oncoming driver is also turning right, it's normally safest to keep the other vehicle to your right and turn behind it. If you have to pass in front of the other vehicle, take extra care as your view may be obscured.

A box junction – indicated by yellow hatched lines – should be kept clear. Only enter it if your exit road is clear. You may wait in the box if you want to turn right and are only prevented from doing so by oncoming traffic.

HC 174

D 6

At crossroads where there aren't any signs or markings, no-one has priority. Check very carefully in all directions before you proceed.

HC 146

Roundabouts are designed to aid the flow of traffic. Follow signs and road markings as you approach and negotiate these. Normally, if you're going straight ahead

D 8

HC 186-187

- don't signal as you approach
- signal left before you leave the roundabout, just after you pass the exit before the one you want.

D 8

Some vehicles may not follow the normal rules:

- cyclists and horse riders may stay in the left-hand lane even if they're turning right
- long vehicles may take up a different position to stop the rear of the vehicle hitting the kerb.

Overtaking, turning and reversing

HC
163

D
7

Overtaking is a dangerous manoeuvre. Ask yourself if you really need to overtake and never do so if you're in any doubt as to whether it's safe.

HC
137-138

D
7

You should normally overtake on the right, but in a one-way street you can overtake on either side. Take extra care if you're overtaking on a dual carriageway, as the right-hand lane can also be used by traffic turning right.

IF YOU'RE ON A BUSY ROAD AND FIND THAT YOU'RE TRAVELLING IN THE WRONG DIRECTION KEEP GOING UNTIL YOU CAN FIND A QUIET SIDE ROAD IN WHICH TO TURN ROUND SAFELY"

HC
200

D
5 + 9

If you're on a busy road and find that you're

- travelling in the wrong direction
- in the wrong lane at a busy junction

keep going until you can find somewhere safe, such as a quiet side road, in which to turn round.

Never reverse

- for longer than is necessary
- from a side road into a main road.

HC
200-203

D
9

When reversing into a side road always check road and traffic conditions in all directions (you may remove your seat belt while reversing if it helps you get a better view). If you're not sure that it's safe, get out and check before you start to reverse. The greatest hazard to passing traffic is when the front of your vehicle swings out.

Crossings

If someone is standing on the pavement, waiting to cross at a zebra crossing, stop, as long as it's safe to do so, and let them cross.

HC
195-199

D
7

KYTS
122

Pelican crossings are light controlled. When the red light changes to flashing amber, wait for any pedestrians to get clear of the crossing before moving off.

On toucan crossings, cyclists are allowed to cycle across at the same time as pedestrians walk.

Level crossings

A level crossing, where a railway line crosses the road, may have countdown markers to warn you if the crossing is hidden, such as round a bend.

HC
293, p109

D
6

KYTS
26-29

- If the warning lights come on as you're approaching the crossing – stop
- If you're already on the crossing when the warning lights come on or a bell rings – keep going and clear the crossing
- If you're waiting at a level crossing, a train has passed but the red lights keep flashing – wait. There may be another train coming.

Stopping and parking

HC 239, p131 ►
D 9 ►
HC 248-250 ►
D 13 ►
HC 240 ►
D 6 ►
HC 242-243 ►

At night, the safest place to park your vehicle is in your garage, if you have one. If you're away from home try to find a secure car park or park in a well-lit area.

If you have to park on a road, you must leave your sidelights on if the speed limit on that road is over 30 mph. Normally park on the left-hand side of the road so other road users can see your reflectors, but in a one-way street you can park on either side.

Never stop on a clearway. On an urban clearway or a road marked with double white lines (even where one of the lines is broken) you may stop only to set down and pick up passengers.

Do not park where you would cause a danger or obstruction to others, such as

- on or near the brow of a hill
- at a bus stop
- opposite a traffic island
- in front of someone else's drive
- near a school entrance
- within 10 metres (32 feet) of a junction (in Northern Ireland, within 15 metres or 48 feet of a junction).

Don't cause an obstruction by stopping or parking where there are restrictions such as yellow lines and associated signs. In a controlled parking zone you'll have to pay to park. Park within marked bays on the days and times shown on the zone entry signs.

Only park in a disabled parking space if you or your passenger are a disabled badge holder. Remember to display the badge when you leave the vehicle.

HC
238, 245

D
6

KYTS
45

"AT NIGHT, THE SAFEST PLACE TO PARK YOUR VEHICLE IS IN A WELL-LIT AREA"

FAQs

What do I do if there's an obstruction on my side of the road?

D
7

Give way to oncoming traffic if there isn't room for you both to continue safely.

"ON A DUAL CARRIAGEWAY, IF A SIGN WARNS THAT MY LANE WILL CLOSE 800 YARDS AHEAD, MOVE TO ANOTHER LANE IN GOOD TIME – DON'T LEAVE IT UNTIL THE LAST MINUTE"

HC 288-289 ▶
D 11 ▶

On a dual carriageway, if a sign warns that my lane will close 800 yards ahead, when should I move over?

Move to another lane in good time – don't leave it until the last minute.

HC 115 ▶

At night, if a car overtakes me, when should I dip my headlights?

Dip your lights as soon as the car passes you or your lights could dazzle the other driver.

HC 155 ▶
D 10 ▶

I'm on a road that's only wide enough for one vehicle and there's a car coming towards me. What do I do?

Pull into a passing place on your left, or if the nearest passing place is on your right, wait opposite it.

How can brake lights give signals to other drivers?

Brake lights show traffic behind that you're slowing down.

◄ D 5

What do I do if I want to turn right onto a dual carriageway that has a narrow central reservation?

Wait until the road is clear in both directions or you'll obstruct traffic coming from your right.

◄ HC 173
◄ D 8

Are there times when I have to stop by law?

Yes. You must stop

- *when involved in an accident*
- *at a red traffic light*
- *when signalled to do so by a police officer, VOSA officer, or school crossing patrol.*

◄ HC 105, 109, 286

In a well-lit built-up area, can I drive using sidelights only?

It's recommended that you use dipped headlights so that you can be seen easily by others.

◄ HC 115

11 Road and traffic signs

Signs

HC
109

D
6

KYTS
9

You MUST comply with all traffic signs and road markings. Road signs can be divided into groups depending on their shape and colour. Each group means something different:

- circular signs give orders
  - blue circles give an instruction
  - red rings or circles tell you what you must not do
- triangular signs give warnings
- rectangular signs give information.

The exception to the shape rule is the 'stop' sign – this is octagonal to give it greater prominence and ensure that its meaning is understood even if partly obscured, say by snow.

HC
p106

KYTS
20

Maximum speed limit signs are shown by red circles – you must not exceed the speed shown. National speed limits (given on page 63) apply where no specific speed limits are indicated. Speed limit signs may be incorporated in other signs, such as those indicating a traffic-calmed area.

"MARKINGS ON THE ROAD GIVE INFORMATION, ORDERS OR WARNINGS. AS A GENERAL RULE, THE MORE PAINT, THE MORE IMPORTANT THE MESSAGE"

It's impossible to mention all the signs in this small book. *Know Your Traffic Signs* shows all the signs that you're likely to come across and *The Highway Code* contains important advice and instructions surrounding current GB Legislation and best practice in road safety. It's important that you familiarise yourself with these so that you don't inadvertently break the law.

HC
p106-116

KYTS
9-61

KYTS
77-89

Road markings

Markings on the road give information, orders or warnings. As a general rule, the more paint, the more important the message.

Lines along the road can be divided into

HC
127-131

D
6

KYTS
62-4

- those along the middle of the road
  - short broken white lines divide lanes
  - longer broken white lines indicate a hazard ahead: only overtake if the road ahead is clear
  - double white lines with a solid white line on your side of the road – you must not cross or straddle the line (see page 78)
  - white diagonal stripes or chevrons – these separate lanes of traffic or protect traffic turning right

HC
p115-116

D
6

KYTS
62, 65,
122

- those along the side of the road
  - a white line shows the edge of the carriageway
  - yellow lines show waiting and stopping restrictions
  - zigzag lines (white at pedestrian crossings, yellow outside schools) mean no stopping or parking at any time.

HC
p114 + p116

Lines on or across the road

D
6

KYTS
60, 70, 73

- broken lines across the road mean 'give way' (at a roundabout, give way to traffic from the right)
- a solid line means 'stop'
- various markings on the road (give way triangles, road hump markings, arrows) warn of a hazard.

HC
p114-116

KYTS
62-72

As with signs, you should refer to *Know Your Traffic Signs* and *The Official Highway Code* to get the full picture on road markings. Reflective studs may be found on motorways and other roads. These are specially useful at night and when visibility is poor.

HC
132

"YOU FIND RED FLASHINIG LIGHTS AT LEVEL CROSSINGS, LIFTING BRIDGES OR OUTSIDE FIRE STATIONS. STOP WHEN THESE SHOW"

Traffic lights and warning lights

At traffic lights, the sequence of lights and their meaning is

HC
p102

KYTS
119-120

- red – stop and wait behind the stop line
- red and amber – stop and wait
- green – go, if the way is clear
- amber – stop unless you've already crossed the stop line or you're so close to it that pulling up might cause an accident
- red (as above).

There may be a green filter arrow. This means that you can go in the direction of the arrow, even if the main light isn't showing green.

D
6

If the traffic lights are out of order, proceed with great care, as nobody has priority. This problem may be brought to your attention by a sign.

HC
p102

KYTS
13, 26-29,
120

You find red flashing lights at level crossings, lifting bridges or outside fire stations. Stop when these show.

74

On motorways, signals on the overhead gantries or roadside may be accompanied by flashing lights:

- amber – warns you of a hazard (e.g. lane closures, to leave at the next exit, fog) or a temporary maximum speed limit
- red (above your lane) – tells you that the lane is closed beyond this point, so move into another lane
- red (above all the lanes, on the central reservation or roadside) – tells you to stop. You must not go beyond that point in any lane.

HC
255-258, p102
KYTS
89-91

Signals given by drivers and the police

Drivers normally signal their intention to turn by using their indicators. Ensure that your indicators are cancelled after turning to avoid misleading other road users. Be aware that another driver may have left their indicator on by mistake. For example, if you're emerging from a junction and a driver coming along the main road from the right is indicating left, wait until the vehicle starts to turn before you emerge.

HC
103-104
D
5

"ENSURE YOU KNOW ALL ARM SIGNALS AND POLICE SIGNALS IN CASE YOU NEED TO USE THEM"

An arm signal may be used to strengthen or clarify the message, such as when

- signalling to turn right in busy traffic
- slowing down to give way at a zebra crossing.

If you're slowing down and stopping just after a junction, wait to signal until you're passing the junction, or just after it.

HC
p103-104 ▶

Police may signal to you if they're directing traffic.

Ensure you know all arm signals and police signals in case you need to use them.

HC
110-112 ▶
D
5 ▶

The horn may be used to warn others of your presence. It must not be used between 11.30 pm and 7.00 am. Only use your horn when stationary if another vehicle is likely to cause a danger.

The only reason that you should flash your headlights is to warn other road users that you're there.

HC
106 ▶

A police officer following you in a patrol vehicle may flash their headlights, indicate left and point to the left to get you to stop. Pull up on the left as soon as it's safe to do so.

Use of road lanes

HC
140-141,
143 ▶
D
6 ▶
D
11 ▶
KYTS
128-133 ▶

Contraflow lanes are lanes that flow in the opposite direction to the majority of the traffic. Bus and cycle contraflow lanes may be found in one-way streets. They will be signed and marked on the road. Don't enter these lanes.

You may also see contraflow lanes at roadworks. When you see the signs, reduce your speed in good time, choose an appropriate lane early and keep the correct separation distance from the vehicle in front.

HC
264, 268 ▶
D
11 ▶

The right-hand lane of a three-lane motorway is an overtaking lane. Always move back to a lane on your left after overtaking to allow other vehicles to overtake. You may not overtake on your left on a free-flowing motorway or dual carriageway.

"YOU MAY SEE CONTRAFLOW LANES AT ROADWORKS.
WHEN YOU SEE THE SIGNS, REDUCE YOUR SPEED"

FAQs

I've seen some signs with a brown background – does this mean
anything in particular?

Signs with a brown background give tourist information.

KYTS
34, 84,
100-102

Sometimes you see lorries with large arrows on the back. What do
they mean?

*These are placed on slow-moving or stati onary maintenance vehicles which are
blocking traffic lanes. They show you which side of the vehicle you should pass.*

HC
289, p113

HC
129

Can I ever cross double white lines where there's a solid white line on my side of the road?

You can cross a solid white line if you're passing a stationary vehicle or overtaking a pedal cycle, horse or road maintenance vehicle, if they're travelling at 10 mph or less.

HC
116

D
3 + 11

Can I use my hazard warning lights when I'm moving?

If you're driving on a motorway or unrestricted dual carriageway, you can use your hazard warning lights to warn drivers behind you that there's an obstruction ahead.

HC
288

KYTS
136

What different ways can traffic be controlled at roadworks?

Traffic can be controlled by

- *a police officer*
- *traffic lights*
- *a stop-go board.*

12 Documents

Before you can legally drive on a public road, you must have

- a valid tax disc displayed on your vehicle. The vehicle registration documents must be correct and up to date
- a valid driving licence, which must be signed
- proper insurance cover
- a valid MOT certificate if required.

You will not be able to tax your vehicle unless you have a valid MOT certificate and appropriate, current insurance documentation.

◀ HC p122

◀ D 2

Licences

The Vehicle Registration Certificate (V5C) contains details of

- the vehicle (including make, model and engine size)
- the registered keeper.

You, the registered keeper, must notify the licensing authority when you change your vehicle, your name or your permanent address. If you buy a second-hand vehicle notify them immediately of the change of ownership.

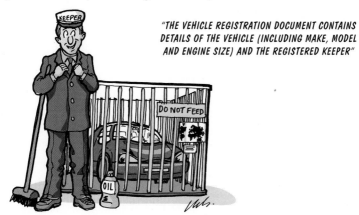

"THE VEHICLE REGISTRATION DOCUMENT CONTAINS DETAILS OF THE VEHICLE (INCLUDING MAKE, MODEL AND ENGINE SIZE) AND THE REGISTERED KEEPER"

◀ HC p122

◀ D 2

A vehicle kept on the public road must have a valid tax disc clearly displayed. This confirms that vehicle excise duty has been paid.

D
2

D
1

HC
p121-122

D
2

HC
p121

D
2

If you do not intend to use your vehicle on the public road, you will not have to pay road tax as long as you advise DVLA in advance. This is called a SORN declaration (Statutory Off Road Notification) and lasts for 12 months.

Before driving on a public road, a learner must have a valid provisional driving licence.

You must notify the licensing authority if

- your health is likely to affect your driving
- your eyesight does not meet the required standard.

Insurance

You must have at least third party insurance cover before driving on public roads. This covers

- injury to another person
- damage to someone else's property
- damage to other vehicles.

Driving without insurance is criminal offence and can lead to a maximum fine of £5000.

You'll need to show your insurance certificate when you're taxing your vehicle or if a police officer asks you for it. You may be issued with a temporary cover note until you receive your insurance certificate.

Before you drive anyone else's vehicle, make sure that the vehicle is insured for your use.

The cost of your insurance depends on many factors, but is generally less if you

- are over 25 years old
- complete the Pass Plus scheme (this is not available in Northern Ireland).

Your insurance policy may have an excess of a certain amount, say £100. This means that you'll have to pay the first £100 of any claim.

The Pass Plus scheme will help newly qualified drivers widen their driving experience and improve basic skills. It may also help to reduce insurance costs.

MOT

Cars must first have an MOT test when they're three years old (four in Northern Ireland).

Trailers and caravans don't need an MOT, but they do need to be kept in good order.

HC p121
D 2

MOT certificates are valid for one year.

You can drive your car without an MOT certificate when driving to an appointment at an MOT centre.

If your vehicle needs an MOT certificate and you don't have one

- you won't be able to renew your road tax
- it could invalidate your insurance.

FAQs

HC p122
D 16

What happens if the police ask to see my documents and I don't have them with me?

You can produce them at a police station within seven days.

HC p123
D 2

If I want to get some practice while I'm learning to drive, can just anyone accompany me?

No, the person accompanying you must be 21 years old and have held (and still hold) a full licence for three years.

HC p127 + p134

I've heard that I'm on probation for two years after I've passed my test, what does this mean?

If you get six or more penalty points within two years of passing your practical test, you'll lose your licence. You'll then have to

- *reapply for a provisional licence*
- *retake your theory and practical tests again.*

Any points on your provisional licence will be transferred onto your new licence when you pass your test.

What is the Pass Plus scheme?

This is a scheme designed to improve your basic driving skills once you have passed your practical driving test. Ask your ADI for details.

81

13 Accidents

Breakdowns

HC
p128 ▶

D
15 ▶

If a warning light on the instrument panel of your vehicle comes on while you're driving, stop (as soon as you can do so safely) and check out the problem.

If your tyre bursts or you've a puncture while you're driving

- hold the steering wheel firmly
- pull up slowly or roll to a stop at the side of the road.

HC
270, 275 ▶

D
15 ▶

If this or any other emergency occurs on a motorway, try to get onto the hard shoulder and call for help from the emergency telephones. The police will answer and ask you

- the phone number
- details of yourself and your vehicle
- whether you belong to a motoring organisation.

HC
278 ▶

A person who has a disability which affects their mobility may display a HELP pennant if they're unable to reach an emergency phone.

"IF YOUR TYRE BURSTS OR YOU'VE A PUNCTURE WHILE YOU'RE DRIVING ON A MOTORWAY, CALL FOR HELP FROM THE EMERGENCY TELEPHONES"

HC
293, 299 ▶

If you break down on a level crossing, get everyone out of the vehicle and clear of the crossing. Then call the signal operator from the phone provided. Only move your vehicle if the operator tells you to do so. If you're waiting at a level crossing and the red light signal continues to flash after a train has gone by, wait, as there may be another train coming.

D
6
KYTS
27

Safety in tunnels

D
7

Before driving through a tunnel remove any sunglasses and switch on dipped headlights. It's particularly important to keep a safe distance from the vehicle in front when driving in a tunnel, even if it's congested.

Look out for variable message signs that warn of accidents or congestion. It's also helpful to tune your radio with the frequency shown.

If your vehicle, or the vehicle in front, is involved in an accident or breaks down in a tunnel

- switch off the engine
- put your hazard warning lights on
- then go and call for help immediately from the nearest emergency telephone point.

If your vehicle catches fire while you are driving through a tunnel, drive it out of the tunnel, if you can do so without causing further danger. If this isn't possible then you should

D
16

- stop
- switch on your hazard warning lights
- try to put out the fire (only if it is a small fire).

Warning others of a breakdown or accident

Use your hazard warning lights

HC
116, 274

- if you need to slow down or stop on a motorway or high-speed road because of an accident or hazard ahead
- when you're broken down or stopped and temporarily obstructing traffic.

D
3, 11,
15 + 16

If you've a warning triangle, place it at least 45 metres (147 feet) behind your vehicle. This will warn other road users that you've broken down. Never use a warning triangle on a motorway.

Stopping at an accident

HC
283
D
16

If you're the first to arrive at the scene of an incident or crash, stop and warn other traffic. Switch on your hazard warning lights. Don't put yourself at risk:

- make sure the emergency services are called as soon as possible
- ensure that the engines of any vehicles at the scene are switched off
- move uninjured people away from the accident scene.

HC
p117
D
16

A vehicle carrying dangerous goods will display an orange label or a hazard warning plate on the back. Report what it says when you call the emergency services. The different plates are shown in *The Highway Code*.

First aid

HC
p131
D
16

Even if you don't know any first aid, you can help any injured people by

- keeping them warm and comfortable
- keeping them calm by talking to them reassuringly
- making sure that they're not left alone.

HC
p131-133
D
16

Don't move them as long as the area is safe. Only move them if they're in obvious danger, and then with extreme care. If a motorcyclist is involved, never remove their helmet unless it's essential in order to keep them alive, because removal of the helmet could cause more serious injury. Always seek medical assistance.

Never offer a casualty a cigarette to calm them down.

There are three vital priorities - ensure a clear airway, check for breathing, and try to stop any heavy bleeding. If someone is unconscious, follow the 'DR ABC' code as follows

D - Danger - check for danger before you approach

R - Response - gently shake the shoulders, check for response

A - Airway - check the airway is clear

B - Breathing - check for breathing for up to 10 seconds

C - Compressions - use two hands in the centre of the chest, press down 4-5cm at a rate of 100 per minute. Use one hand, gently for a small child (2 fingers for an infant).

If they're not breathing, consider giving mouth-to-mouth resuscitation:

- check and if necessary clear their mouth and airway
- gently tilt their head back as far as possible
- pinch their nostrils together.

84

Only stop when they can breathe without help. If the casualty is a small child, breathe very gently. Once the casualty is breathing normally, place them in the recovery position and check the airway to make sure it is clear. Keep checking, and don't leave them alone.

"EVEN IF YOU DON'T KNOW ANY FIRST AID, YOU CAN HELP ANY INJURED PEOPLE BY KEEPING THEM WARM AND COMFORTABLE, KEEPING THEM CALM BY TALKING TO THEM REASSURINGLY AND MAKING SURE THAT THEY ARE NOT LEFT ALONE"

If they're bleeding

- apply firm pressure to the wound
- raise the limb as long as it isn't broken

to help reduce the bleeding.

People at the scene may be suffering from shock. Warning signs include a rapid pulse, sweating and pale grey skin.

- Reassure them constantly
- Keep them warm
- Loosen any tight clothing
- Avoid moving them unless it's necessary
- Make sure they're not left alone.

If someone is suffering from burns

- douse the burns thoroughly with cool non-toxic liquid for at least 10 minutes
- don't remove anything sticking to the burn.

Reporting

If you're involved in an accident, stop. It's an offence not to stop and call the police if any other person is injured or there's damage to another vehicle, property or animal. If you don't do this at the time, you must report the accident to the police within 24 hours (immediately in Northern Ireland).

If another vehicle is involved, find out

- whether the other driver owns the vehicle
- the make and registration number of the vehicle
- the other driver's name, address and telephone number and details of their insurance.

"IF YOU'RE INVOLVED IN AN ACCIDENT WITH ANOTHER VEHICLE, FIND OUT WHETHER THE OTHER DRIVER OWNS THE VEHICLE"

HC
286, p122

The police may ask you to produce, following an accident (or at any other time)

- your insurance certificate
- the MOT certificate for the vehicle you're driving
- your driving licence.

FAQs

HC 280
D 11

What should I do if I see something fall from a lorry on the motorway?

Stop at the next emergency telephone and report the hazard to the police. Do the same if anything falls from your own vehicle – don't try to retrieve it yourself.

"IF YOU SEE SOMETHING FALL FROM A LORRY ON THE MOTORWAY, STOP AT THE NEXT EMERGENCY TELEPHONE AND REPORT IT TO THE POLICE"

What should I do if my engine catches fire?

D 16

Pull up as quickly and safely as possible. Get yourself and any passengers out and away from the vehicle. Then call the fire brigade. Do not open the bonnet as this would make the fire worse

What would you suggest I carry in my car for use in an emergency?

D 16

It's useful to have a first aid kit, a warning triangle and a fire extinguisher. This equipment could be invaluable and is a small price to pay if it helps to prevent or lessen an injury.

What should I do if I smell petrol?

D 16

Stop and investigate as soon as you can do so safely. Don't ignore it. It can be useful to carry a fire extinguisher, which may help in tackling a small fire, but don't take any risks.

14 Vehicle loading

Vehicle stability

You, as a driver, are responsible for making sure that your vehicle isn't overloaded. Overloading can seriously affect the handling, especially steering and braking.

Securely fasten any load carried on a roof rack. A heavy load will reduce the stability of your vehicle.

HC 98
D 2

Passengers

All passengers should wear seat belts if they're fitted. You, as a driver, are responsible for ensuring that all children (under 14 years) wear a suitable restraint. The type of restraint varies with the age of the child. For example, for a child under three years, one of the following is suitable:

HC 100-101
D 2

- a baby carrier
- a harness
- a child seat.

Under no circumstances should a passenger travel in a caravan while it's being towed.

D 19

"UNDER NO CIRCUMSTANCES SHOULD A PASSENGER TRAVEL IN A CARAVAN WHILE IT'S BEING TOWED"

Towing

If you're planning to tow a caravan, it'll help the handling of your vehicle if you have a stabiliser fitted to your towbar. This will help particularly when driving in crosswinds. You can also fit a breakaway cable to the trailer braking system as an additional safety device.

D 19

If a trailer or caravan starts to swerve or snake as you're driving along, ease off the accelerator and reduce your speed gradually to regain control.

HC 98, p40

On a three-lane motorway, towing vehicles are restricted to

D 19

- a 60 mph speed limit
- the left-hand and centre lanes only – they must not use the right-hand lane.

FAQ

Should my tyres always be inflated to the same pressure?

Inflate your tyres to a higher pressure

D 14

- *when you're carrying a heavy load*
- *if you're driving fast for a long distance, such as on a motorway.*

Your vehicle handbook should tell you the correct pressure for different circumstances.

How will I know the maximum weight that can be put on the towbar?

The maximum noseweight which should be applied to your vehicle's towbar can normally be found in the vehicle handbook.

D 19

Revision test one

1   *Mark **one** answer*

You are driving past a line of parked cars. You notice a ball bouncing out into the road ahead. What should you do?

- ⊙ Continue driving at the same speed and sound your horn
- ⊙ Continue driving at the same speed and flash your headlights
- ⊙ Slow down and be prepared to stop for children
- ⊙ Stop and wave the children across to fetch their ball

2   *Mark **three** answers*

Which of the following vehicles will use blue flashing beacons?

- ⊙ Motorway maintenance
- ⊙ Bomb disposal
- ⊙ Blood transfusion
- ⊙ Police patrol
- ⊙ Breakdown recovery

3   *Mark **one** answer*

You are waiting to come out of a side road. Why should you watch carefully for motorcycles?

- ⊙ Motorcycles are usually faster than cars
- ⊙ Police patrols often use motorcycles
- ⊙ Motorcycles are small and hard to see
- ⊙ Motorcycles have right of way

4   *Mark **one** answer*

At an incident it is important to look after any casualties. When the area is safe, you should

- ⊙ get them out of the vehicle
- ⊙ give them a drink
- ⊙ give them something to eat
- ⊙ keep them in the vehicle

5   *Mark **one** answer*

What does this sign mean?

- ⊙ Crossroads
- ⊙ Level crossing with gate
- ⊙ Level crossing without gate
- ⊙ Ahead only

6 *Mark **one** answer*

It can help to plan your route before starting a journey. Why should you also plan an alternative route?

⊙ Your original route may be blocked

⊙ Your maps may have different scales

⊙ You may find you have to pay a congestion charge

⊙ Because you may get held up by a tractor

7 *Mark **one** answer*

A red traffic light means

⊙ you must stop behind the white stop line

⊙ you may go straight on if there is no other traffic

⊙ you may turn left if it is safe to do so

⊙ you must slow down and prepare to stop if traffic has started to cross

8 *Mark **one** answer*

What does this sign mean?

⊙ Distance to parking place ahead

⊙ Distance to public telephone ahead

⊙ Distance to public house ahead

⊙ Distance to passing place ahead

9 *Mark **one** answer*

When driving in falling snow you should

⊙ brake firmly and quickly

⊙ be ready to steer sharply

⊙ use sidelights only

⊙ brake gently in plenty of time

10 *Mark **one** answer*

You are having difficulty finding a parking space in a busy town. You can see there is space on the zigzag lines of a zebra crossing. Can you park there?

⊙ No, unless you stay with your car

⊙ Yes, in order to drop off a passenger

⊙ Yes, if you do not block people from crossing

⊙ No, not in any circumstances

Where may you overtake on a one-way street?

- Only on the left-hand side
- Overtaking is not allowed
- Only on the right-hand side
- Either on the right or the left

You see two elderly pedestrians about to cross the road ahead. You should

- expect them to wait for you to pass
- speed up to get past them quickly
- stop and wave them across the road
- be careful, they may misjudge your speed

You are driving on a motorway. The traffic ahead is braking sharply because of an incident. How could you warn traffic behind you?

- Briefly use the hazard warning lights
- Switch on the hazard warning lights continuously
- Briefly use the rear fog lights
- Switch on the headlights continuously

Motorcyclists should wear bright clothing mainly because

- they must do so by law
- it helps keep them cool in summer
- the colours are popular
- drivers often do not see them

Driving with under-inflated tyres can affect

- engine temperature
- fuel consumption
- braking
- oil pressure

At a crossroads there are no signs or road markings. Two vehicles approach. Which has priority?

- Neither of the vehicles
- The vehicle travelling the fastest
- Oncoming vehicles turning right
- Vehicles approaching from the right

17 *Mark one answer*

You are planning a long journey. Do you need to plan rest stops?

⊙ Yes, you should plan to stop every half an hour

⊙ Yes, regular stops help concentration

⊙ No, you will be less tired if you get there as soon as possible

⊙ No, only fuel stops will be needed

18 *Mark one answer*

When traffic lights are out of order, who has priority?

⊙ Traffic going straight on

⊙ Traffic turning right

⊙ Nobody

⊙ Traffic turning left

19 *Mark one answer*

You are overtaking a motorcyclist in strong winds? What should you do?

⊙ Allow extra room

⊙ Give a thank you wave

⊙ Move back early

⊙ Sound your horn

20 *Mark three answers*

Excessive or uneven tyre wear can be caused by faults in which THREE of the following?

⊙ The gearbox

⊙ The braking system

⊙ The accelerator

⊙ The exhaust system

⊙ Wheel alignment

⊙ The suspension

21 *Mark one answer*

A friend wants to help you learn to drive. They must be

⊙ at least 21 and have held a full licence for at least one year

⊙ over 18 and hold an advanced driver's certificate

⊙ over 18 and have fully comprehensive insurance

⊙ at least 21 and have held a full licence for at least three years

22 *Mark one answer*

What does this sign mean?

⊙ Buses turning

⊙ Ring road

⊙ Mini-roundabout

⊙ Keep right

When emerging from junctions, which is most likely to obstruct your view?

⊙ Windscreen pillars

⊙ Steering wheel

⊙ Interior mirror

⊙ Windscreen wipers

Anti-lock brakes are most effective when you

⊙ keep pumping the foot brake to prevent skidding

⊙ brake normally, but grip the steering wheel tightly

⊙ brake promptly and firmly until you have slowed down

⊙ apply the handbrake to reduce the stopping distance

Which of these signs shows that you are entering a one-way system?

⊙   ⊙

⊙   ⊙

What is the shortest overall stopping distance on a dry road at 60 mph?

⊙ 53 metres (175 feet)

⊙ 58 metres (190 feet)

⊙ 73 metres (240 feet)

⊙ 96 metres (315 feet)

While driving, this warning light on your dashboard comes on. It means

⊙ a fault in the braking system

⊙ the engine oil is low

⊙ a rear light has failed

⊙ your seat belt is not fastened

You are travelling at the legal speed limit. A vehicle comes up quickly behind, flashing its headlights. You should

⊙ accelerate to make a gap behind you

⊙ touch the brakes sharply to show your brake lights

⊙ maintain your speed to prevent the vehicle from overtaking

⊙ allow the vehicle to overtake

29
*Mark **one** answer*

You are on a motorway. What colour are the reflective studs on the left of the carriageway?

- ⊙ Green
- ⊙ Red
- ⊙ White
- ⊙ Amber

30
*Mark **one** answer*

A driver pulls out of a side road in front of you. You have to brake hard. You should

- ⊙ ignore the error and stay calm
- ⊙ flash your lights to show your annoyance
- ⊙ sound your horn to show your annoyance
- ⊙ overtake as soon as possible.

31
*Mark **three** answers*

Which THREE of the following will affect your stopping distance?

- ⊙ How fast you are going
- ⊙ The tyres on your vehicle
- ⊙ The time of day
- ⊙ The weather
- ⊙ The street lighting

32
*Mark **one** answer*

When you see a hazard ahead you should use the mirrors. Why is this?

- ⊙ Because you will need to accelerate out of danger
- ⊙ To assess how your actions will affect following traffic
- ⊙ Because you will need to brake sharply to a stop
- ⊙ To check what is happening on the road ahead

33
*Mark **one** answer*

You are driving over a level crossing. The warning lights come on and a bell rings. What should you do?

- ⊙ Get everyone out of the vehicle immediately.
- ⊙ Stop and reverse back to clear the crossing
- ⊙ Keep going and clear the crossing
- ⊙ Stop immediately and use your hazard warning lights

What should you do as you approach this overhead bridge?

- Move out to the centre of the road before going through
- Find another route, this is only for high vehicles
- Be prepared to give way to large vehicles in the middle of the road
- Move across to the right hand side before going through

You are towing a caravan. Which is the safest type of rear-view mirror to use?

- Interior wide-angle mirror
- Extended-arm side mirrors
- Ordinary door mirrors
- Ordinary interior mirror

How does alcohol affect you?

- It speeds up your reactions
- It increases your awareness
- It improves your co-ordination
- It reduces your concentration

Which vehicle might have to use a different course to normal at roundabouts?

- Sports car
- Van
- Estate car
- Long vehicle

You have just driven out of fog. Visibility is now good. You MUST

- switch off all your fog lights
- keep your rear fog lights on
- keep your front fog lights on
- leave fog lights on in case fog returns

You are following a long vehicle approaching a crossroads. The driver signals right but moves close to the left-hand kerb. What should you do?

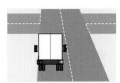

- Warn the driver of the wrong signal
- Wait behind the long vehicle
- Report the driver to the police
- Overtake on the right-hand side

40 *Mark one answer*

What is the national speed limit for cars and motorcycles in the centre lane of a three-lane motorway?

⊙ 40 mph
⊙ 50 mph
⊙ 60 mph
⊙ 70 mph

41 *Mark one answer*

How should you overtake horse riders?

⊙ Drive up close and overtake as soon as possible
⊙ Speed is not important but allow plenty of room
⊙ Use your horn just once to warn them
⊙ Drive slowly and leave plenty of room

42 *Mark three answers*

You have broken down on a motorway. When you use the emergency telephone you will be asked

⊙ for the number on the telephone that you are using
⊙ for your driving licence details
⊙ for the name of your vehicle insurance company
⊙ for details of yourself and your vehicle
⊙ whether you belong to a motoring organisation

43 *Mark one answer*

You want to turn right from a main road into a side road. Just before turning you should

⊙ cancel your right-turn signal
⊙ select first gear
⊙ check for traffic overtaking on your right
⊙ stop and set the handbrake

44 *Mark two answers*

Overloading your vehicle can seriously affect the

⊙ gearbox
⊙ steering
⊙ handling
⊙ battery life
⊙ journey time

45 *Mark one answer*

Your vehicle has broken down on a motorway. You are not able to stop on the hard shoulder. What should you do?

⊙ Switch on your hazard warning lights
⊙ Stop following traffic and ask for help
⊙ Attempt to repair your vehicle quickly
⊙ Stand behind your vehicle to warn others

46

*Mark **three** answers*

Driving long distances can be tiring. You can prevent this by

- ⊙ stopping every so often for a walk
- ⊙ opening a window for some fresh air
- ⊙ ensuring plenty of refreshment breaks
- ⊙ completing the journey without stopping
- ⊙ eating a large meal before driving

47

*Mark **one** answer*

At an incident a casualty is unconscious but still breathing. You should only move them if

- ⊙ an ambulance is on its way
- ⊙ bystanders advise you to
- ⊙ there is further danger
- ⊙ bystanders will help you to

48

*Mark **one** answer*

An Emergency Refuge Area is an area

- ⊙ on a motorway for use in cases of emergency or breakdown
- ⊙ for use if you think you will be involved in a road rage incident
- ⊙ on a motorway for a police patrol to park and watch traffic
- ⊙ for construction and road workers to store emergency equipment

49

*Mark **one** answer*

The conditions are good and dry. You could use the 'two-second rule'

- ⊙ before restarting the engine after it has stalled
- ⊙ to keep a safe gap from the vehicle in front
- ⊙ before using the 'Mirror-Signal-Manoeuvre' routine
- ⊙ when emerging on wet roads

50

*Mark **one** answer*

At which type of crossing are cyclists allowed to ride across with pedestrians?

- ⊙ Toucan
- ⊙ Puffin
- ⊙ Pelican
- ⊙ Zebra

Revision test two

1 *Mark **one** answer*

Anti-lock brakes are of most use when you are

⊙ braking gently
⊙ driving on worn tyres
⊙ braking excessively
⊙ driving normally

2 *Mark **one** answer*

Which sign means there will be two-way traffic crossing your route ahead?

⊙ 　⊙

⊙ 　⊙

3 *Mark **one** answer*

Unbalanced wheels on a car may cause

⊙ the steering to pull to one side
⊙ the steering to vibrate
⊙ the brakes to fail
⊙ the tyres to deflate

4 *Mark **one** answer*

In which of these situations should you avoid overtaking?

⊙ Just after a bend
⊙ In a one-way street
⊙ On a 30 mph road
⊙ Approaching a dip in the road

5 *Mark **one** answer*

You are joining a motorway. Why is it important to make full use of the slip road?

⊙ Because there is space available to turn round if you need to
⊙ To allow you direct access to the overtaking lanes
⊙ To build up a speed similar to traffic on the motorway
⊙ Because you can continue on the hard shoulder

You enter a road where there are road humps. What should you do?

- ⊙ Maintain a reduced speed throughout
- ⊙ Accelerate quickly between each one
- ⊙ Always keep to the maximum legal speed
- ⊙ Drive slowly at school times only

By avoiding busy times when travelling

- ⊙ you are more likely to be held up
- ⊙ your journey time will be longer
- ⊙ you will travel a much shorter distance
- ⊙ you are less likely to be delayed

A bus has stopped at a bus stop ahead of you. Its right-hand indicator is flashing. You should

- ⊙ flash your headlights and slow down
- ⊙ slow down and give way if it is safe to do so
- ⊙ sound your horn and keep going
- ⊙ slow down and then sound your horn

Which of these signs means the end of a dual carriageway?

⊙   ⊙

⊙   ⊙

You are driving along a country road. A horse and rider are approaching. What should you do?

- ⊙ Increase your speed
- ⊙ Sound your horn
- ⊙ Flash your headlights
- ⊙ Drive slowly past
- ⊙ Give plenty of room
- ⊙ Rev your engine

What style of driving causes increased risk to everyone?

- ⊙ Considerate
- ⊙ Defensive
- ⊙ Competitive
- ⊙ Responsible

12 *Mark **four** answers*

Which FOUR of these would be indicated by a triangular road sign?

- ⊙ Road narrows
- ⊙ Ahead only
- ⊙ Low bridge
- ⊙ Minimum speed
- ⊙ Children crossing
- ⊙ T-junction

13 *Mark **one** answer*

Other drivers may sometimes flash their headlights at you. In which situation are they allowed to do this?

- ⊙ To warn of a radar speed trap ahead
- ⊙ To show that they are giving way to you
- ⊙ To warn you of their presence
- ⊙ To let you know there is a fault with your vehicle

14 *Mark **one** answer*

Before starting a journey it is wise to plan your route. How can you do this?

- ⊙ Look at a map
- ⊙ Contact your local garage
- ⊙ Look in your vehicle handbook
- ⊙ Check your vehicle registration document

15 *Mark **one** answer*

To avoid spillage after refuelling, you should make sure that

- ⊙ your tank is only three quarters full
- ⊙ you have used a locking filler cap
- ⊙ you check your fuel gauge is working
- ⊙ your filler cap is securely fastened

16 *Mark **one** answer*

You are invited to a pub lunch. You know that you will have to drive in the evening. What is your best course of action?

- ⊙ Avoid mixing your alcoholic drinks
- ⊙ Not drink any alcohol at all
- ⊙ Have some milk before drinking alcohol
- ⊙ Eat a hot meal with your alcoholic drinks

17 *Mark **one** answer*

You are driving towards this left-hand bend. What dangers should you be aware of?

- ⊙ A vehicle overtaking you
- ⊙ No white lines in the centre of the road
- ⊙ No sign to warn you of the bend
- ⊙ Pedestrians walking towards you

What does Eco-safe driving achieve?

⊙ Increased fuel consumption

⊙ Improved road safety

⊙ Damage to the environment

⊙ Increased exhaust emissions

You are driving in heavy rain. Your steering suddenly becomes very light. You should

⊙ steer towards the side of the road

⊙ apply gentle acceleration

⊙ brake firmly to reduce speed

⊙ ease off the accelerator

You are entering an area of roadworks. There is a temporary speed limit displayed. You should

⊙ not exceed the speed limit

⊙ obey the limit only during rush hour

⊙ ignore the displayed limit

⊙ obey the limit except at night

Whilst driving, the fog clears and you can see more clearly. You must remember to

⊙ switch off the fog lights

⊙ reduce your speed

⊙ switch off the demister

⊙ close any open windows

You are on a well-lit motorway at night. You must

⊙ use only your sidelights

⊙ always use your headlights

⊙ always use rear fog lights

⊙ use headlights only in bad weather

What does this sign mean?

⊙ Through traffic to use left lane

⊙ Right-hand lane T-junction only

⊙ Right-hand lane closed ahead

⊙ 11 tonne weight limit

What does this sign mean?

⊙ School crossing patrol

⊙ No pedestrians allowed

⊙ Pedestrian zone – no vehicles

⊙ Zebra crossing ahead

25 *Mark **three** answers*

Overtaking is a major cause of collisions. In which THREE of these situations should you NOT overtake?

⊙ If you are turning left shortly afterwards

⊙ When you are in a one-way street

⊙ When you are approaching a junction

⊙ If you are travelling up a long hill

⊙ When your view ahead is blocked

26 *Mark **one** answer*

The left-hand lane of a motorway should be used for

⊙ breakdowns and emergencies only

⊙ overtaking slower traffic in the other lanes

⊙ slow vehicles only

⊙ normal driving

27 *Mark **one** answer*

At some traffic lights there are advance stop lines and a marked area. What are these for?

⊙ To allow cyclists to position in front of other traffic

⊙ To let pedestrians cross when the lights change

⊙ To prevent traffic from jumping the lights

⊙ To let passengers get off a bus which is queuing

28 *Mark **one** answer*

A toucan crossing is different from other crossings because

⊙ moped riders can use it

⊙ it is controlled by a traffic warden

⊙ it is controlled by two flashing lights

⊙ cyclists can use it

29 *Mark **one** answer*

You are waiting to emerge at a junction. Your view is restricted by parked vehicles. What can help you to see traffic on the road you are joining?

⊙ Looking for traffic behind you

⊙ Reflections of traffic in shop windows

⊙ Making eye contact with other road users

⊙ Checking for traffic in your interior mirror

30 *Mark **one** answer*

You are approaching a mini-roundabout. The long vehicle in front is signalling left but positioned over to the right. You should

⊙ sound your horn

⊙ overtake on the left

⊙ follow the same course as the lorry

⊙ keep well back

*Mark **two** answers*

You are the first to arrive at the scene of a crash. Which TWO of these should you do?

- ⊙ Leave as soon as another motorist arrives
- ⊙ Make sure engines are switched off
- ⊙ Drag all casualties away from the vehicles
- ⊙ Call the emergency services promptly

32   *Mark **one** answer*

You are trying to move off on snow. You should use

- ⊙ the lowest gear you can
- ⊙ the highest gear you can
- ⊙ a high engine speed
- ⊙ the handbrake and footbrake together

33   *Mark **one** answer*

You are on a road that has no traffic signs. There are street lights. What is the speed limit?

- ⊙ 20 mph
- ⊙ 30 mph
- ⊙ 40 mph
- ⊙ 60 mph

34   *Mark **two** answers*

You have just passed your practical test. You do not hold a full licence in another category. Within two years you get six penalty points on your licence. What will you have to do?

- ⊙ Retake only your theory test
- ⊙ Retake your theory and practical tests
- ⊙ Retake only your practical test
- ⊙ Reapply for your full licence immediately
- ⊙ Reapply for your provisional licence

35   *Mark **one** answer*

You are following a vehicle at a safe distance on a wet road. Another driver overtakes you and pulls into the gap you have left. What should you do?

- ⊙ Flash your headlights as a warning
- ⊙ Try to overtake safely as soon as you can
- ⊙ Drop back to regain a safe distance
- ⊙ Stay close to the other vehicle until it moves on

36
*Mark **one** answer*

You are following a large lorry on a wet road. Spray makes it difficult to see. You should

- ⊙ drop back until you can see better
- ⊙ put your headlights on full beam
- ⊙ keep close to the lorry, away from the spray
- ⊙ speed up and overtake quickly

37
*Mark **one** answer*

You are driving towards this level crossing. What would be the first warning of an approaching train?

- ⊙ Both half barriers down
- ⊙ A steady amber light
- ⊙ One half barrier down
- ⊙ Twin flashing red lights

38
*Mark **one** answer*

You are about to drive home. You feel very tired and have a severe headache. You should

- ⊙ wait until you are fit and well before driving
- ⊙ drive home, but take a tablet for headaches
- ⊙ drive home if you can stay awake for the journey
- ⊙ wait for a short time, then drive home slowly

39
*Mark **one** answer*

Why is it particularly important to carry out a check on your vehicle before making a long motorway journey?

- ⊙ You will have to do more harsh braking on motorways
- ⊙ Motorway service stations do not deal with breakdowns
- ⊙ The road surface will wear down the tyres faster
- ⊙ Continuous high speeds may increase the risk of your vehicle breaking down

40
*Mark **three** answers*

When you are moving off from behind a parked car you should

- ⊙ look round before you move off
- ⊙ use all the mirrors on the vehicle
- ⊙ look round after moving off
- ⊙ use the exterior mirrors only
- ⊙ give a signal if necessary
- ⊙ give a signal after moving off

You are dazzled at night by a vehicle behind you. You should

- ⊙ set your mirror to anti-dazzle
- ⊙ set your mirror to dazzle the other driver
- ⊙ brake sharply to a stop
- ⊙ switch your rear lights on and off

You are on a motorway. A large box falls onto the road from a lorry. The lorry does not stop. You should

- ⊙ go to the next emergency telephone and report the hazard
- ⊙ catch up with the lorry and try to get the driver's attention
- ⊙ stop close to the box until the police arrive
- ⊙ pull over to the hard shoulder, then remove the box

You intend to turn right into a side road. Just before turning you should check for motorcyclists who might be

- ⊙ overtaking on your left
- ⊙ following you closely
- ⊙ emerging from the side road
- ⊙ overtaking on your right

You are approaching this roundabout and see the cyclist signal right. Why is the cyclist keeping to the left?

- ⊙ It is a quicker route for the cyclist
- ⊙ The cyclist is going to turn left instead
- ⊙ The cyclist thinks The Highway Code does not apply to bicycles
- ⊙ The cyclist is slower and more vulnerable

You have to treat someone for shock at the scene of an incident. You should

- ⊙ reassure them constantly
- ⊙ walk them around to calm them down
- ⊙ give them something cold to drink
- ⊙ cool them down as soon as possible

46   *Mark **one** answer*

You will see these red and white markers when approaching

- ⊙ the end of a motorway
- ⊙ a concealed level crossing
- ⊙ a concealed speed limit sign
- ⊙ the end of a dual carriageway

47   *Mark **one** answer*

Your vehicle is parked on the road at night. When must you use sidelights?

- ⊙ Where there are continuous white lines in the middle of the road
- ⊙ Where the speed limit exceeds 30 mph
- ⊙ Where you are facing oncoming traffic
- ⊙ Where you are near a bus stop

48   *Mark **one** answer*

You are driving on a motorway. You have to slow down quickly due to a hazard. You should

- ⊙ switch on your hazard lights
- ⊙ switch on your headlights
- ⊙ sound your horn
- ⊙ flash your headlights

49   *Mark **two** answers*

Which TWO should you allow extra room when overtaking?

- ⊙ Motorcycles
- ⊙ Tractors
- ⊙ Bicycles
- ⊙ Road-sweeping vehicles

50   *Mark **one** answer*

Why would you fit a stabiliser before towing a caravan?

- ⊙ It will help with stability when driving in crosswinds
- ⊙ It will allow heavy items to be loaded behind the axle
- ⊙ It will help you to raise and lower the jockey wheel
- ⊙ It will allow you to tow without the breakaway cable

Answers test one

1	Slow down and be prepared to stop for children	**26**	73 metres (240 feet)
2	Bomb disposal	**27**	a fault in the braking system
	Blood transfusion	**28**	allow the vehicle to overtake
	Police patrol	**29**	Red
3	Motorcycles are small and hard to see	**30**	ignore the error and stay calm.
4	keep them in the vehicle	**31**	How fast you are going
5	Crossroads		The tyres on your vehicle
6	Your original route may be blocked		The weather
7	you must stop behind the white stop line	**32**	To assess how your actions will affect following traffic
8	Distance to parking place ahead	**33**	Keep going and clear the crossing
9	brake gently in plenty of time	**34**	Be prepared to give way to large vehicles in the middle of the road
10	No, not in any circumstances	**35**	Extended-arm side mirrors
11	Either on the right or the left	**36**	It reduces your concentration
12	be careful, they may misjudge your speed	**37**	Long vehicle
13	Briefly use the hazard warning lights	**38**	switch off all your fog lights
14	drivers often do not see them	**39**	Wait behind the long vehicle
15	fuel consumption	**40**	70 mph
	braking	**41**	Drive slowly and leave plenty of room
16	Neither of the vehicles	**42**	for the number on the telephone that you are using
17	Yes, regular stops help concentration		for details of yourself and your vehicle
18	Nobody		whether you belong to a motoring organisation
19	Allow extra room	**43**	check for traffic overtaking on your right
20	The braking system	**44**	steering
	Wheel alignment		handling
	The suspension	**45**	Switch on your hazard warning lights
21	at least 21 and have held a full licence for at least three years	**46**	stopping every so often for a walk
22	Mini-roundabout		opening a window for some fresh air
23	Windscreen pillars		ensuring plenty of refreshment breaks
24	brake promptly and firmly until you have slowed down	**47**	there is further danger
25		**48**	on a motorway for use in cases of emergency or breakdown
		49	to keep a safe gap from the vehicle in front
		50	Toucan

Answers test two

1	braking excessively	26	normal driving
2		27	To allow cyclists to position in front of other traffic
		28	cyclists can use it
3	the steering to vibrate	29	Reflections of traffic in shop windows
4	Approaching a dip in the road	30	keep well back
5	To build up a speed similar to traffic on the motorway	31	Make sure engines are switched off
			Call the emergency services promptly
6	Maintain a reduced speed throughout	32	the highest gear you can
7	you are less likely to be delayed	33	30 mph
8	slow down and give way if it is safe to do so	34	Retake your theory and practical tests
9			Reapply for your provisional licence
		35	Drop back to regain a safe distance
		36	drop back until you can see better
10	Drive slowly past	37	A steady amber light
	Give plenty of room	38	wait until you are fit and well before driving
11	Competitive	39	Continuous high speeds may increase the risk of your vehicle breaking down
12	Road narrows	40	look round before you move off
	Low bridge		use all the mirrors on the vehicle
	Children crossing		give a signal if necessary
	T-junction	41	set your mirror to anti-dazzle
13	To warn you of their presence	42	go to the next emergency telephone and report the hazard
14	Look at a map	43	overtaking on your right
15	your filler cap is securely fastened	44	The cyclist is slower and more vulnerable
16	Not drink any alcohol at all	45	reassure them constantly
17	Pedestrians walking towards you	46	a concealed level crossing
18	Improved road safety	47	Where the speed limit exceeds 30 mph
19	ease off the accelerator	48	switch on your hazard lights
20	not exceed the speed limit	49	Motorcycles
21	switch off the fog lights		Bicycles
22	always use your headlights	50	It will help with stability when driving in crosswinds
23	Right-hand lane closed ahead		
24	Zebra crossing ahead		
25	If you are turning left shortly afterwards		
	When you are approaching a junction		
	When your view ahead is blocked		

Competition Rules

The following rules apply to this competition. By entering this competition, entrants will be deemed to have accepted these rules and to agree to be bound by them.

1. Only one entry will be accepted per purchase of Theory Test Extra - the official DSA Guide.
2. All entries must be on original official entry forms. No photocopies will be accepted.
3. Entries must be received by the Promoter by no later than 5.00pm on Monday, 7 September 2009 (**Closing Date**). Entries must be submitted by ordinary post to the Promoter's free mailing address at: TSO, Freepost, ANG 4748, Norwich, NR3 1YX.
4. The competition will run from 21 July 2008 to 7 September 2009 and one prize shall be awarded to a winner chosen from valid entries received by the Promoter by the Closing Date. No responsibility can be taken by the Promoter for lost, late, misdirected or stolen entries.
5. The prize awarded to the winner will be one car (not necessarily the car pictured), being either a Peugeot 206 1.4 3 door Petrol model or another make and model of approximate equivalent value (£8995 at the time of these rules going to press) to be selected by the Promoter in its absolute discretion. Colour is subject to availability. Insurance and all on the road charges are not included and will be the winner's responsibility. There will be one prize only and accordingly only one winner. The prize cannot be transferred or exchanged and there is no cash alternative.
6. Only entrants over the age of 17 and resident in the United Kingdom are eligible to enter the competition. The Promoter reserves the right to request evidence of proof of age and residence from the winner before any prize will be awarded.
7. The winning entry will be decided by the judges in their absolute discretion from correct entries submitted by eligible entrants received by the Closing Date. A "correct" entry means a fully completed entry, with the first three questions answered correctly, the most apt and original essay and otherwise in compliance with these rules.
8. The winner will be notified by 23 September 2009. Only the winner will be contacted personally via the email address or telephone number they provide.
9. If the winner cannot be contacted by the means provided, the Promoter reserves the right to have the judges decide on an alternative winner from other correct entries received by the Closing Date, using the same criteria as for the original "winner" and subject to these rules.
10. The winner's name will be published on the Promoter's website at www.tso.co.uk on or about 23 September 2009 for a period of approximately 60 days.
11. The prize will be made available within six weeks of the Closing Date by arrangement between the Promoter and the winner, provided that the Promoter shall not be responsible for any delivery costs.
12. By entering this competition, an entrant agrees that if they accept any Prize, they will be deemed to consent to:
    (a)   the use for promotional and other purposes (without further payment and except as prohibited by law) of their name, city/town/county of residence, likeness and Prize information; and
    (b)   participate in the Promoter's reasonable marketing and promotional activities.
    The entrant agrees that all rights including copyright in all works created by the entrant as part of the competition entry shall be owned by the Promoter absolutely without the need for any payment to the entrant. They further agree to waive unconditionally and irrevocably all moral rights pursuant to the Copyright, Designs and Patents Act of 1988 and under any similar law in force from time to time anywhere in the world in respect of all such works.
13. No entries will be returned to entrants by the Promoter. Therefore, entrants may wish to retain a copy.
14. The Promoter reserves the right to cancel this competition or amend these rules at any stage without prior notice, if deemed necessary in its opinion, especially if circumstances arise outside of its control. Any such cancellation or changes to the rules will be notified on the Promoter's website.
15. This competition is not open to employees or contractors of the Promoter or the Driving Standards Agency or any person directly involved in the organisation or running of the competition, or their direct family members. Any such entries will be invalid.
16. By entering this competition, entrants warrant that all information submitted by them is true and correct and that they are eligible and have legal capacity to enter this competition. The Promoter reserves the right to disqualify any entrant if it has reasonable grounds to believe that the entrant has breached these rules.
17. Any personal data provided in any entry will be dealt with by the Promoter in accordance with the requirements of the Data Protection Act 1998, provided that the winner expressly consents to the information set out in rule 12(a) being used in the manner specified therein.
18. The judges' and the Promoter's decisions in relation to any aspect of this competition are final and no correspondence will be entered into. Neither the judges nor the Promoter will have any liability to any person in relation to their decisions or any damage, loss, injury or disappointment suffered arising from the competition (except to the extent that such liability cannot be limited or excluded by law).
19. The competition and these rules shall be governed by English law.
20. The "Promoter" means The Stationery Office Limited, St Crispins, Duke Street, Norwich, NR3 1PD (the publishers of The Official DSA Learner Range). The judges will be employees of the Promoter.

THEORY TEST EXTRA

the OFFICIAL DSA GUIDE

2009 WIN A CAR COMPETITION*

TSO, DSA's official publishing partner, is offering you the chance to win a new car.

To enter, simply answer the questions and tell us in 25 words or less how learning to drive will make a difference to your life. The winner will be the entrant who answers the first 3 questions correctly and writes the most apt and original 25 word essay, as decided by the judges.

Please send the entry form to: Win a Car Competition, TSO, Freepost, ANG 4748, Norwich, NR3 1YX (No stamp required).

1. What is the nearest distance in metres you may park to a junction?

....

2. When may you wait in a box junction?

....

3. You have driven through a flood. What is the first thing you should do?

....

Tie Breaker: Learning to drive will change my life.... (complete in 25 words or less)

....

....

....

....

When are you planning/ hoping to take your theory test?

Within a fortnight ☐ Within a month ☐ In 1-3 months ☐ In 3-6 months ☐
In 6-12 months ☐ In 12+ months ☐

When are you planning/ hoping to take your practical test?

Within a fortnight ☐ Within a month ☐ In 1-3 months ☐ In 3-6 months ☐
In 6-12 months ☐ 12+ months ☐

Do you already own a car?

Yes ☐ No ☐

If Yes, is the car...

New ☐ Second-hand ☐

Do you plan to buy a car when you pass?

Yes ☐ No ☐

If Yes, will the car be...

New ☐ Second-hand ☐

Name of shop or website that you bought this product from?

....

How would you improve this, or any other DSA product?

....

....

Name ....

Address ....

.... Date of birth ....

...

Daytime tel. .... Email ....

Mobile tel. ....

TSO (The Stationery Office) Ltd is proud to be DSA's official publishing partner

Prices, images and publication dates are correct at time of going to press but may be subject to change without notice.

Account holders should note that all credit card transactions will not be shown on their statements. The personal information provided here will only be used to process your order and keep you informed of related products or services. We will not pass your data on to any third parties.

TSO would like to continue to keep you informed of products and services that may be of interest to you. If you do not wish to receive these updates in future please let us know.

I do not want to receive these updates from TSO in future ☐

I have read, accept and agree to be bound by the Competition Rules

Signature .... Date ....

If you would like us to send you email updates on your specific area(s) of interest register at www.tsoshop.co.uk/signup.

* Terms and conditions apply